DO ANTS HAVE
ARSEHOLES?

DO ANTS HAVE ARSEHOLES?

. . . and 101 other bloody ridiculous questions

From the popular 'Corrections & Clarfications' page of *Old Git* magazine

JON BUTLER *and* BRUNO VINCENT

Penny, do remember to change this!

sphere

With many thanks to Camilla Elworthy

SPHERE

First published in Great Britain in 2007 by Sphere

A CIP catalogue record for this book
is available from the British Library.

ISBN 978-0-7515-4041-3

Papers used by Sphere are natural, recyclable products made from
wood grown in sustainable forests and certified in accordance
with the rules of the Forest Stewardship Council.

Typeset in Transitional by M Rules
Printed and bound in Great Britain by
Clays Ltd, St Ives plc
Paper supplied by Hellefoss AS, Norway

Sphere
An imprint of
Little, Brown Book Group
100 Victoria Embankment
London EC4Y 0DY

An Hachette Livre UK Company

www.littlebrown.co.uk

An Introduction by the Editor

The *Old Git* may be a venerable publication, an historical one in fact, but it has never been a *Young Git*. From the moment of its conception, some time between five and six in the evening – as its creator Phospot Smallblanes-Styveson-Bestface looked down over Gower Street and saw some sportive medical students juggling kidneys for money and thought to himself, The world's going to hell – our journal has been a home for more sensible and settled minds in a world where so often newness and excitement seem in danger of overwhelming common sense, decency and good, solid conservatism.

Of course since its first issue the journal has had some rocky times. I am not shy of cover stories past which have seemed (with the help of hindsight) imprudent. 'Indians Naturally Subservient, Study Shows' (Nov 1849), 'Mosley For P.M.! Black Shirt Fashion Special' (Aug 1936) and 'Ice Caps to Cover Earth by Year 2007' (Jan 1970) are among them. But our strong suit has been making a home for right-thinking writers with something to say rather than boat-rockers bent on personal glory.

Our 'Corrections & Clarfications' page [*Penny, I know you have a blind spot for the word 'clarfications' – do be sure not to replicate the misprint in the masthead when you come to type this up*] has been running since 1941 when the old git in charge, Sir Godfrey Phlegming, posed what he thought to be a rhetorical question about the efficacy of contraceptives made from fine bone china. Such a flood of articulate and considered responses did his staff receive that he was persuaded to set up a questions and answers page and his secretary (who turned out to be a Nazi paratrooper posing as an aged, crippled washer-woman) elected to publish the three or four most ignorant, absurd or infuriating exchanges. This tradition has been upheld by all the secretaries to have followed in Fräulein Schencker's footsteps. Only three editors have succeeded Phlegming, each achieving an extraordinary old age in their tenure. I followed on from old Hal 'Haphazard' Hammondsley when he succumbed to a hang-gliding accident on a jaunt with Bill Deedes in 1991, aged 102, well may he rest. And at a frisky sixty-nine I look forward to several decades [*unless you cause me a relapse of the Chinese Trots, Penny. I hope you're not introducing new typos into my carefully chosen wrods*] of enjoyable editorship.

While we revere old-fashioned values, I hope we are not entirely ignorant of new trends and language – so, if you'll excuse me, I hope you 'love up' our first collection of readers' learned responses to the questions thrown up by everyday life and that it makes you 'go down' on our organ!

Tiddly spanks!

The Editor

Are there any undiscovered colours?

– question courtesy of Sir Michael Cummings, Biggin Hill

I have been furiously mixing paints ever since this question appeared in last month's issue, and am astonished and proud beyond measure to be able to announce that I have discovered what I believe to be an entirely new colour! By mixing blue paint and red paint, I have come up with a wonderfully rich, regal hybrid that is somehow warmer and more mellow than blue, and cooler and more elegant than red. I call it 'Simon', because my name is in fact Simon. I am enclosing a swatch of pure Simon for you to reproduce in your magazine – perhaps on the cover??!?

SIMON SAYERS, COUNTY DURHAM

[Ed note: We're not entirely sure, Simon, but we think you might have made purple. Thanks for trying, though.]

Not to be disrespectful, but this could very well serve as a kind of prototypical stupid question, much as Donald Rumsfeld's words about 'known knowns' and 'unknown unknowns' have become bywords for political bluster and obfuscation. The way the human eye reacts to the light it receives determines the colours we see. A point often made is that we can never be sure that while we agree something is 'brown', we are seeing the same colour. In theory I might receive a blow to the head and wake up seeing completely different (or 'new') colours but never know the difference.

Synaesthesia is interesting in its implications for this – it results mostly from neurological trauma. In the USSR one Yuri Zherkov survived a plane crash near Katerinapol and afterwards saw colours in musical notes. Taken to the National Soviet Gallery, he was able to play many of the great paintings there in astonishing improvised arrangements on the piano. He had always been tone deaf, however, and his later attempts to paint the great Russian composers' works were met with critical revulsion, official anger and banishment to a Gulag for anti-Soviet aesthetic tendencies, where he died of potato poisoning.

GREG MARESH, CUBBLING, ALASKA

What was the best thing before sliced bread?

Simone Taylor, London

Wooden legs, stout, second wives, the King James Bible, iron bridges, public executions, hot acorns at the theatre, the London Bridge and Queen Anne's tits are among the things that have been historically referred to as 'the best

4

thing since'. Many other verbatim references are to be found among letter-writers, diarists and journalists to 'the worst thing since': the Black Death, Welsh whores, that bastard Cromwell, France, the French, French anything, German anything (foreign anything, in fact), window tax, the Industrial Revolution and, in Pepys's famous words, 'the law against buggery'.

TERRY GRAITE, HOLYHEAD, WALES

We in the Best Thing Since Society have spent years campaigning for something to replace sliced bread in the 'best thing since' stakes. We are hopeful of recognition through avenues such as this column, so that people might start to call various things the 'best thing since . . .' Here is a selection of our current alternatives: resealable coffee packets, the suck-nipple on bottled water, cashback, the 'recall email' facility on Microsoft Outlook, Snake II, multi-region DVD players, Orange Wednesdays and the *Daily Telegraph* Giant General Knowledge Crossword.

JEREMY SHRIMP, BEST THING SINCE SOCIETY, LAND'S END

As ousted chair of the Best Thing Since Society, reading Mr Shrimp's facile suggestions, I thought it might illuminate your readers to see the other things that were once considered for entry by that pathetic organisation: the Concorde, Gary Glitter, the widget, audio cassettes, Madonna getting into movies, leg warmers, spam, Tony Blair, the Northern Line, medium-wave radio, boxed wine, modernism, postmodernism and the Cup Winners' Cup.

It will be apparent how transient the appeal of each of these things was. Yet sliced bread remains with us, as useful as ever.

JONATHAN RADIOHEAD, NEXT BEST THING SINCE SOCIETY,
BOULDER, COLORADO

This question was most interesting to me, as a former baker by trade. The best thing before sliced bread, was having ordinary, unsliced bread and a full set of f*cking fingers.

HARRY NOEL, WEST TITTERING, SHROPS

When signmakers go on strike, how do they make their point?

Joost Kuyt, Amsterdam

As Mr Herring recounted in his fascinating letter (January issue), striking signmakers make their point precisely by not carrying signs (though as some commentators have identified, the whole affair consequently seems like nothing so much as twenty blokes in overalls, looking cross). Further to earlier answers, I remember well the pitched battles between signmakers and militant coal miners in the summer of 1984. When members of the south Derbyshire colliery appeared over the hill, carrying home-made banners decrying Thatcher's government, a chilling cry of 'SCABS!' went up from the five striking signmakers, and a bloody skirmish ensued, while the police – grateful for the chance of a cup of tea – looked on.

ALBERT SHANKLY, LANGLEY MILL, NOTTS

I am very interested to read the letter of Monsieur Shankly about signmakers who make riots in England in the 1980s. Of course, in France the union of signmakers, FROTAGE (*Fédération Régionale des Ouvriers Textuels/Artisans en Grève*), we do things very differently, and with much more class. We do carry signs, but instead of the angry slogan, our signs they feature beautiful paintings of the signmakers themselves, in the style of M. René Magritte, over the legende: *Ceci n'est pas un fabricant des signes*. Though, I confess, we also block all of the roads into Paris and firebomb the houses of old womens.

JEAN-MARIE ORANAIS, PARIS

Every day I'm surrounded by people who talk but don't listen to each other. Has anyone ever calculated what percentage of conversation is actually understood, or listened to?

J. Box, Hereford

I know that my gran, who talked incessantly for eighty years, was shocked when my granddad died and an autopsy revealed he'd been deaf from birth. She didn't talk much after that.

I. BEECHES, BRIGHTON

I don't know whether this has been calculated, but a few readers might recall this story about people not listening from a few years ago. In the late nineties an abandoned lighthouse was reopened on the supposedly uninhabited Orkney island of Muckle Green Holm. It was found to contain the remains of Percy Bentwhite, an army deserter and passionate radio ham, who had spent his inheritance stacking the lighthouse with equipment to record for posterity everything broadcast by the BBC. When the archive (which ran to tens of millions of feet of tape) was analysed, countless programmes were recovered – we have Bentwhite to thank for many early episodes of *Hancock's Half Hour*.

Among these were the completely unknown broadcasts of Archie Spector, who hosted the *Night Service* on the BBC's Third Programme in the late forties and early fifties. Spector began by asking listeners for their music requests, but when he received no reply, he quickly lost heart and, intuiting that no one was listening, his professionalism began to go downhill. Within a month he was reading his diary out, detailing a tortured love for a girl called Maisie. He began to fantasise, visiting his deepest sexual depravities on her. Still uncensured, perhaps out of desperation he recounted his entire life story, month by month, in Proustian detail. This lasted three years. By the time he finished he was certainly insane. He began committing lewd acts in public parks and crowing about his crimes over the air to an unheeding police force. Struck with remorse, he read the entire Bible, and wept for a fortnight afterwards. He said nothing for three weeks except 'Johann Sebastian Bach'. He wrote his own soap opera set in a Scottish castle and acted out all the parts, including one with his own name, for which he chose the harsh, grating tones of an old Greek woman. Then for six months he abandoned human speech and expressed himself through sounds he could perform in the studio: clapping, screaming, stamping, vomiting into boxes, even bringing himself to a very convincing orgasm. His career in broadcasting ended when the *Night Service* was abandoned suddenly and arbitrarily in 1953, though he went on to serve for thirty years as the Conservative MP to Kingston and Surbiton.

STEVE THEW, COUNTY DOWN

How many men would it take to kill an elephant with their bare hands?

Jessica Hair, Melbourne, Australia

I presume, naturally, that any men involved in such a titanic struggle would be naked, their bronzed young bodies glistening in the fierce African sun. Many years ago, before I went up to Oxford, I found myself in just such a situation with Carruthers, who had been my faithful fag throughout the trials and tribulations of Big School. Driving through the northern expanses of Kenya in my uncle's handsome Derby Bentley, enjoying the cool, spiced smoke of a Sullivan cigarillo, I was at once shocked to see the road ahead blocked by the huge, terrible silhouette of a bull elephant. Hello, what brave fellow is this? I asked, turning to Carruthers, who had turned the same shade of ash as the Bentley's plush grey crocodile seating . . .

GENERAL SMYTHINGTON-SMYTHE, DORSET, ENGLAND

[Ed note: General Smythington-Smythe's correspondence goes on for many pages. To summarise: by his reckoning as a military man, it would take at least a hundred naked, oiled men to subdue an elephant: one to distract it with iced buns and peanuts, two to poke it in the eye, and the other ninety-seven to bite its tail and hindquarters until it died through loss of blood, confusion and stress. Penny, would you be a dear and get me a cup of tea before typing this 'Ed note' up for the journal? There's a girl.]

Who gets to name the 'Dulux' colour chart?

Stella Remmington, Bognor

Sadly, Mrs Trump's rather fanciful answer (May issue) about the Dulux Old English sheepdog mascot sniffing coloured cards, and urinating at random on flashcard words, is false – though I concede that might explain the baffling 'Placebo Jizz Party' that adorned many an English sitting room in the summer of 1983. The truth, I'm sorry to report, is somewhat duller: the genius behind the naming of Dulux's colour chart is – or at least, *was* – the renowned chromatologist and bon viveur Derek Larousse, a heavy-set Frenchman with an enormous nose, wild, untamed eyebrows and a passion for breeding otters. Larousse made his name on the international colour circuit in the 1970s, dating a steady stream of top French starlets and transforming the fortunes of Dulux with literally scores of daring new shades that reflected the classiest brands and trends of the period – 'Blue Nun Bleu' and the envelope-pushing 'Coq Sportif' (a dangerously enflamed pink) being the most famous. From there, as we now know, the maestro's stock fell sharply. Accused by peers of selling out in the 1980s (having broadened his scope to the naming of pharmacy goods, chocolate biscuits and Bob Geldof's children), nobody really knows where Larousse is or if his work continues.

Or perhaps we do know, after all. Amid the Magnolias, Tuscan Reds and Sunshine Yellows that fill the shelves of

DIY stores across the country, a practised eye may still spot the rakish mark of the master in the bestselling paint 'Red Mimsy' (nothing to do with the recent blockbuster erotic film *The Last Mimzy*); the winner of the Cheltenham Gold Cup 'Pays de Cons'; and in various feminine hygiene products, the best known of which is, to quote the whispered advert voiceover, the 'secret treatment for secret ladies' places', 'VAGICLOT' (to rhyme with 'sew').

MICHEL ARGOT, NANTES

Further to earlier published answers, it's not often remembered that Andy Warhol prepared his own colour chart for a short-lived exhibition at the famous Thievers Street Studio in 1969 called simply 'Colour Chart'. He bought tins of paint from a New York hardware store and painted bland oblongs of them around the room, accompanied by their definition. The exhibition notes replicate the exhibition itself in the form of a colour chart and read thusly:

Grey: Brains
Yellow: Yellow
Red: Suffragette
Black: Man
White: Richard Nixon
Pale Blue: Desert
Pale Yellow: Dessert
Bright Pink with Orange Dots: Long Division
Skull on a Black Background: Poison
The Mona Lisa: Bored

The exhibition did not do well, and closed after two weeks.

JAMIE THEFFERT, CREWE

Do ants have arseholes?

Brad Nematode, Oklahoma City

Although it has been rendered useless by evolution, contrary to popular belief the humble ant *does* have an arsehole. It is, in fact, the smallest orifice in any known creature, so tiny that it only allows a single atom to pass at a time. The sound of an ant breaking wind has been recorded as the lowest decibel-level achievable in nature (Prof. Humbert Unself created a fake ant entirely from porcelain which emitted a quieter one). The farts are, however – although silent – quite incredibly violent, and have accounted for many a fainting fit in university biology departments down the years.

DR DAVID POWELL-STROPES, EMERITUS PROFESSOR,
DEPTARTMENT OF GAS RESEARCH, DUNDEE UNIVERSITY

Powell-Stropes's learned answer has great implications for classicists such as myself. In the well-known Greek myth, the architect and engineer Daedalus was presented with an apparently unsolvable puzzle by King Minos: feed a fine piece of thread through the spiral centre of a helical seashell, and win riches beyond measure. As the tale is usually told, Daedalus cleverly tied the string to the back leg of an ant, and tempted it to walk through the helix in search of a single bead of honey placed at the other end of the shell. Or at least, that is how most scholars have got around the tricky – seemingly insurmountable – riddle presented by the original Greek:

αυφωΩέά ϊωψέυ
έυ ωΩέ έά
αυυανέά ωψυ
φω

And so cunning Daedelus,
Tricked strong-armed Minos
Threading the ant's tiny arsehole
Like a needle

Since ants were not known to have arseholes until Powell-Stropes's research was published in this organ, the original version was simply ignored in favour of a much more believable solution, viz. the tying of a knot around the fabulous ant's back leg.

PROF. CLIVE LADYWELL, DEPARTMENT OF GREEK STUDIES,
MERTON COLLEGE, OXFORD

W here does my lap go, when I stand up? And can I have it back?

Becky Innes, Holloway, London

Lapland.

ANONYMOUS, LAPLAND

I can't believe that the previous answer actually came from Lapland. The 'Lapps' are an ancient, literal-minded race, so-named by the nineteenth-century Swedish ethno-linguist Per Blonquist because the Lapp language affords no way of expressing the concept of a 'lap' at all. In Lapp society if someone spills a glass of wine during dinner, the wine is said to have landed 'on their genitals'. Similarly TV dinners are eaten 'off one's crotch', and caution must be taken when offering a temporary seat for a small child on a train. Indeed, such is the consequent linguistic taboo surrounding this area of a Lapp's anatomy that, over the centuries, they took to wearing modesty-preserving napkins pinned over their crotch at all times. This so tickled Blonquist back in 1873 that the placing of a napkin on the lap before eating dinner became something of an overnight trend throughout the great cities of northern Europe (a whim that now appears to be simply the height of good manners).

EVA ANDERSSON, GOTHENBERG

Are 'crabs' related to crabs?

Mrs Mary Beeston, Stapleford, Notts

I'm sure that a biologist would say 'no'. However, when my husband returned with 'crabs' from his annual work conference in Eastbourne, I can report that he moved sideways rapidly, turned red and screamed when the pan of boiling water hit him, so perhaps they're not so different after all.

EMILY DRINKWELL, DOVER

What a fascinating question – indeed they are not. But many of the more mysteriously shaped sea creatures are related to human-borne parasites. The hairlouse, for example, was in the Pleistocene era a large creature that could burrow through mountains and eat trees whole. What we know as the jellyfish was earlier a type of genital wart to be found on larger whales, which broke free and developed independent life. And even earlier, the humble ant was as large as a current-day walrus and would wallow in mud pits – so large, in fact, it had parasites of its own, one of which, *Paracletus parnassus*, resided in the warm moist cleft of its backside and would develop into the modern jaguar.

JACOB L'ARRIVISTE, ARCHOLE, LOUISIANA

I have no idea about the natural history of crabs, but I would like fellow readers to learn from my terrible mistake, which ruined my sister's wedding day. For the record, 'crab paste' from the chemist's is intended to be smeared on your crotch, to kill pubic lice. 'Crab paste' from the supermarket tastes considerably better in sandwiches.

CASEY FINK, VANCOUVER

I s laughter the best medicine?

Rafaela Romaya, Tunbridge Wells

As any student of comedy will tell you, laughter can be our instinctive reaction to almost any emotion – shock, embarrassment, fear, relief, hatred, happiness or love. We have found that even those trying to cope with the most appalling diseases are comforted by being shown the Robin Williams movie *Patch Adams*. They find it helps to reflect that there are still things in this world more horrible than whatever awaits them.

B. BAYERLING & Q. STEMPT, ST MICHEL'S HOSPICE, AMSTERDAM

Further to earlier answers, I must report a funny story that my grandfather were fond of telling, about the opening of the first ever fried chicken shop, in the centre of Leeds in 1755, by his great-great-grandfather, the fierce, redoubtable

Colonel John 'Rooster' Saunders (no relation to his now-famous namesake). He were quite the showman, Saunders – folk say he paid for twelve stout local lads to dress up in large, garish chicken suits and flap about outside on the pavement, calling customers in to sample a bucket (in them days, it were literally a wooden four-gallon bucket) of chicken wings and a free pot of pickled eggs (mayonnaise – and, therefore, coleslaw – wasn't invented until the following year, in France).

One of the lads, worse for wear after a night at the card table, is said to have overbalanced as he clucked about because of his big chicken head – and stumbled into the street, where he were immediately struck by a passing shire horse. The boy lay in the dust, dazed, so the story goes, and were holding his wing like he'd broken it. In them days of course, it could take a good hour for the doctor's wagon to arrive, so the lad's mates set about making him more comfortable where he lay, keeping his spirits up until help came. At that moment, my great-great-great-great-grandfather – never one to have much patience with shirkers – is said to have come out of his shop, his face turning a dark, splotched purple, and barked: 'Why in God's name did that bloody chicken cross t'road?'

At this, the wounded boy is said to have laughed heartily, which must surely have eased his pain. Mind you, the story goes on to tell that old Rooster, bridling at having been laughed at by a mere boy, did not stop there, and paid for the Navy to press-gang the lad into service. Clearly, laughter was not much use to his health in the long run, since his joke ultimately landed him in Nelson's service, where he died horribly under cannon fire during the notorious Nicaraguan set-to of 1780.

JOSH BUNSWORTHY, LEEDS, ENGLAND

As a youthful-looking single woman in her early fifties who works as a nurse in the burns unit of the Derby Royal Infirmary, I'm delighted to be able to tell your readers that laughter really can help patients to recover faster. I pride myself on my 'GSOH' – I love to laugh, go to the theatre, and socialise with friends – and my patients always tell me how much it cheers them up to see me around the wards at night. All I need now is a tall, dark, handsome man to take me on long walks in the country, to have fun with and maybe more; now that really would be a tonic!

GRACE BLANCHFLOWER, DERBY, ENGLAND

What's in a name?

Christina Schweppe, Cologne, Germany

For my hard-earned shilling, Grace Blanchflower seems quite the most becoming name I have read these past fifty years, and the person who bears it strikes this humble reader's mind's eye as quite perfectly fitting her name's delicate beauty. As a nimble, tennis-playing sixty-seven-year-old who loves country walks, perhaps she would like to join him for one? (A country walk that is, naughty.)

EDWARD O. PINKLY, SWEEDTHORPE, DERBS

Some would say, nothing. Others – my wife and I included – would disagree most vigorously.

MR AND MRS REGINALD C*NT, BRECON BEACONS, WALES

Mr and Mrs C*nt either have a very unusual name or are being coy about its correct spelling. This reminds me of my great-grandfather's embarrassment as a translator in the brief peace talks which preceded the Zulu war in 1879. As the only isiZulu-speaking English officer, he was chief intermediary between the tribal leaders and the English army. However, a strict Victorian upbringing, bowdlerisation of literary texts and a mother who considered the erection of Nelson's column an ungodly abomination, meant that he could not bring himself to utter the names of the tribe dignitaries in full, betraying his position with cowardice by annotating them in Roman script as F*ckulu, C'n'l'ng's, and Chief M'sh(gw)h:gaw-a? (we don't know if this last one began life as a rude word or not).

The peace talks were going well until my great-grandfather's shyness caused the English generals to so horribly mispronounce the names (C'n'l'ng's pronounced with all four apostrophes translates into isiZulu as Man Who Pisses On Wife to Try Make Pregnant) that the Battle of Isandlwana followed in days. My great-grandfather died during the side-action at Rorke's Drift, upon which the movie *Zulu* is based, and was one of the only men there (living and dead alike) not to be honoured for bravery, as he was found with a spear clean through his dictionary and his heart, in a bran tub, where he had hidden when the action started.

BERTIE BOLLOCKS-BROWN, FOULNESS

As noted in the *Book of Heroic Failures*, by common consent the worst name recorded in England was Depressed Cupboard Cheesecake, who was born to (depressed) parents in 1972. Depressed is a friend of mine, and we've always agreed that not changing an unfortunate name shows strength of character.

SADDAM BUTTPLUG, TEWKESBURY

This is a question that has plagued the Spastics Society for much of its existence. After decades of children labelling each other 'spastics' if they showed any signs of a speech defect, it changed its name to Sparks. Within months teachers noticed that the new playground insult was 'Sparks kid'. It would seem its only chance to prevent adding a new insult to the language by a further name change would be to change its name to the Freaks Society.

HOLLY-ANNA BUMFACE, NICE, FRANCE

What's in a name? Nothing much according to the creators of this column, who in over a thousand editions have failed to spell the word 'clarifications' correctly.

GERALD BUTTER, INTEGUMENT HOLDINGS, CARSHALTON

[Ed note: Penny, DO please address this problem. I've been asking you for over two years now to retype the heading, and at least 50 per cent of the mailbag we receive from the cretins who read the Old Git *consists of letters asking if we've noticed that 'clarfications' is itself in need of correction. You have pretty ankles, Penny, but you're no typist. Lapsang souchong! And lots of it.]*

Is it a biological coincidence, or a matter of function, that my index finger fits perfectly in my nostrils, my ears and my bumhole?

Stuart Rod, Barking

A similar, though somewhat more restrained version of this question has already been answered to most scientists' satisfaction by the bestselling book *Why Don't Penguins' Feet Freeze* (the phenomenon is, I'm afraid, simply a happy coincidence – at least, for all of us out there with small fingers). However, *Old Git* regulars might be tickled by the extraordinary real-life story of Hans Keffle, 'the Human Ocarina', who made millions in the freak shows of the American Midwest by employing precisely this quirk of biology to musical effect. Keffle's act really was quite something, if contemporary newspaper reports are to be believed. He insisted on performing naked, with coloured balloons expertly used to protect his modesty. Lovers of classical music might be interested to know that in order to reach the nine high 'C's demanded by Donizetti's operatic aria 'Pour mon âme', he had to take off his wristwatch.

SAM HARKER, ILLINOIS

If your finger fits 'perfectly' into your bumhole, Stuart, then I'm sorry for your family and any people you may have dated over the years. I would seek a doctor's advice as soon as possible, and in the meantime invest in a small cork.

ADAM MANDERSSON, REYKJAVIK

🐜 🐜 🐜

Has the snow come early in Moscow this year?

Colonel Sir Geoffrey Beezewater, Lambeth (South Bank), UK

As a frequent traveller to Moscow and a keen amateur meteorologist, I can assure the Colonel that the snow has indeed come early in that fine city this year. As a result I can confirm that the bluebird has flown the nest. Repeat, the bluebird has flown the nest!

T. STARLING, UNADDRESSED ENVELOPE, HAND DELIVERED

Indeed, the bluebird has flown. But the nest was empty. Perhaps the starling instructed him to look in the wrong nest *again*? The Colonel might consider training his starlings a little better.

A. BLUEBIRD, UNADDRESSED ENVELOPE, HAND DELIVERED

The bluebird, it occurs to the starling, has laid his droppings over the entire enterprise. If the starling sees

23

him at the water bowl the starling may be inclined to peck him in the eye. It's a wonder he flew the nest at all without bonking his head on a branch and knocking himself out.

T. STARLING, UNADDRESSED ENVELOPE, HAND DELIVERED

The bluebird respectfully points out it was the starling who ballsed up the switch in Budapest. Eton and Trinity College Cambridge and he can't read a bloody map. Perhaps he would have better luck if he removed his beak from his arse.

A. BLUEBIRD, UNADDRESSED ENVELOPE, HAND DELIVERED

According to the lore of the Sioux, the eagle used to rest upon a high branch and say: small birds must remember not to expose themselves to prey by petty squabbling. The bluebird has done well in the circumstances. The starling is the only bird with the experience for the job. They have been placed on the same branch for a reason.

COLONEL SIR GEOFFREY BEEZEWATER, LAMBETH (SOUTH BANK), UK

I really do hate to sound like an old fuddy-duddy, but I'm afraid I don't believe that the above correspondents have any practical experience of the habits of birds at all. I have been birdwatching for forty years and have never seen any of the behaviour that these gentlemen describe. Bluebirds and starlings do not cooperate with each other in any way, and a starling pecking out a bluebird's eye is quite impossible, but the idea that a starling could get its head trapped in its backside is so grotesquely fictitious that it compelled me to write in. I do hope your editors can monitor the level of accuracy in future replies with more rigour.

JAMES CUNYNGHAM, COLDING, BORDERS

[Ed note: if you think we're fact-checking all this crap that comes in, sunshine, you're dumber than we thought. Penny, write up the PC version of this and insert, you dear little thing – and perhaps don't include my preamble this time, mm? My wife was less than impressed by my complimenting you on your – really, strikingly well-made – ankles, earlier on.]

I would love to know what your readers think I should do with my hair. It is naturally very curly; and bizarrely, the longer it gets, the tighter the curls become – with the result that the actual volume of my hair seen from a distance appears to be exactly the same. Should I cut it?

Chantal Magnicourt, Chamonix

What an interesting question! Speaking as a physicist, your hair represents a remarkable small-scale model of the very creation of the universe itself. If we use the equation

$Z\lambda = Y2/(2)^2$, where λ is the speed of light, Z is the mass of a single proton and Y is infinity, we can show that, given an infinite number of years, your hairstyle would achieve an infinitely small, infinitely dense mass; to whit, a black hole. Maddeningly, however, nobody would be able to appreciate the terrible, Medusan beauty of your hair, since the event horizon – your forehead – would capture light itself.

PROFESSOR JOHN F. SMURF, AREA 51, NEVADA

Who cares? For I am in love. Oh Edward, our countryside picnic in the soft sunset glow of the yellow oilseed flowers was divine – I feel so silly for worrying about your curious note inviting me to a 'Rape Date'! You dear, funny old man. And the trip to the whisky distillery, and the beautiful convent overlooking the rugged Derbyshire peaks . . . Do the nuns *really* force themselves to do press-ups in a cucumber field as a trial of faith? I never know when you're teasing me, you silly creature! But I haven't laughed so hard in years, and all of my patients say that I have an extra glow in my cheeks since we met. Can I see you again?

GRACE BLANCHFLOWER, DERBY, ENGLAND

What does 'titfink' mean?

Barry Knowles, Blackpool

The titfink is a charming, brightly coloured Scandinavian bird, whose mournful song can be heard on moonlit winter nights. The name, of course, comes from the bird's call: a chirruping, quarrelsome teet-fink! teet-fink!

LARS KLUBFOOT, PAJALA, SWEDEN

Mr Klubfoot's answer is obviously wrong. Titfink is a Swedish word, but much ruder than he suggests. It is the sensation aroused in a person (so common in Sweden) as they are uncuffed after kinkysex. The fiddliness of unlocking the notoriously poorly designed Finnish handcuffs (it can often take five minutes) brings to the Swede a realisation of the humiliation and meaninglessness of what they have done. At this moment, the temperature falling fast, the Swede can be expected to exclaim, 'Titfink!'

The word crosses over into Norwegian too. It affords Scandinavians especial amusement that the more repressed translators of Ibsen's *A Doll's House* always have Torvald calling Nora his little 'chipmunk', rather than what the original text says.

HENRIK JOHL-KELPERSEN, GOTHENBURG

'Titfink' is not a word at all. Bloody Swedes.

MONTY LE ROUX, BERKS, ENGLAND

Grace! My little titfink. You're right, of course – I have played tennis with the nuns for years, and they made the same playful joke to me about cucumbers when I first met them, over a leisurely half-time lemon barley water. Sister Margaret has a wicked sense of humour – and a fearsome forehand smash. But, Grace – you know, don't you, that it is over between us. You perspicaciously discerned that I have been rapidly gaining weight these last few weeks – and, alas, I wish I could say that it was because of a few too many whiskies. Your bright, shining innocence has shamed me into coming clean, dear lady. My moobs – my 'mitties', as you so delightfully called them – are real. I am a woman, Grace, and that is only the half of it. I believe myself to be three months pregnant. The father is another reader of the *Old Git*, and he is a good man – the masterful General Smythington-Smythe. We are in love, and we intend to be married, before covering both ourselves and England in glory by breaking the all-comers record for elderly births held by the sixty-six-year-old Spaniard, Maria del Carmen Bousada de Lara. I am sorry if you are hurt by this news, Grace. You're a game filly, and you deserve a real man. I hope that you will find him soon, while I remain respectfully, your

ENID O'PINKLEY, SWEEDTHORPE, DERBYS

How can you mend a broken heart?

Grace Blanchflower, Derbyshire

Don't be fooled by 'Enid' O'Pinkley. He's no woman, Grace – he's a serial philanderer who has long used the pages of the *Old Git* as his personal rutting ground. Rest assured that the net is finally closing in on the old rake. Let this letter serve as notice, O'Pinkley: we're watching you. For the record, Grace, perhaps some of my grandmother's wisdom will help you: the best way to get *over* someone, is to get *under* someone. Might I interest you in a game of whist, sometime soon?

MICHAEL O'HOOLIHAN, RAMSGATE

[Ed note: Right, enough of this. Moobs? MITTIES? The whole thing is descending into a Roman orgy, Penny. Or at least the sort of greasy romp one can expect in one of those overpriced east London massage parlours. Either way, it's becoming awfully hot in here. Is there any more Apple Tango in the refrigerator?]

A curious question this – since the actual sensation of having one's 'heart' broken, in my experience, is more akin to a hard, wet punch in the gut. You need to get over your pain, Miss Blanchflower, and get over it fast. Readers might like to know that some indigenous cultures are far more hard-nosed than our own, as evidenced by the Native American proverb 'The dam is built; no more beavers for you', a phrase which forces the rejected brave to see the ridiculousness of his situation, and move on.

For those in need of a more scientific approach, they might do worse than to travel to India in search of top cardiologist Dr Rajiv Patel, who famously performed open-heart surgery on himself after he discovered that his wife had been having it away with the country's top lung man, Dr Sachin Singh. The *Lancet* is unclear on whether Patel's surgery had the desired effect, but he did fall in love with the intensive-care nurse who helped him through the following bedridden year, so perhaps love does conquer all, whichever road we take to get over a broken heart.

TIM KRAKOW, NEVADA

Everyone knows about Walt Disney having his brain frozen, but my boyfriend worked at the Tampa Cryo-Center in Florida one summer and discovered various organs frozen for posterity that you wouldn't expect. Winston Churchill's sinuses were there, along with Charlie Chaplin's pancreas and a part of Errol Flynn I wouldn't even like to mention. One day the boys were playing football in the walk-in freezer and a bad throw made Martin Luther King's heart shatter against a thermostat. They patched it up as good as they could with tape and string, but when the family comes to reclaim it in future generations they're gonna be pissed . . .

HANNAH STEENBURG, MIAMI

What are the benefits of smoking?

Hugo Tipping, London

None whatever. My father, who was a devastatingly handsome B-movie matinée idol through the fifties and sixties encountered both Humphrey Bogart and Steve McQueen in the various jobs he took. Both reached a status of extraordinary fame, as sex symbols and eternal movie icons. Yet both were cut off in their prime by cigarettes. But Daddy, who was John Ford's first choice to play the corpse of the sheriff in John Ford's *They Ride at Dawn*, is still with us, age ninety-seven. Who's the winner there?

JOSEPH L. MARLBOROUGH, CALIFORNIA

Is it possible to fall into a barrel of shit and come up smelling of roses?

Henry Gaylord, Twickenham

The simple answer is, of course, 'no'. However, older readers may recall with a smile watching a young Peter

Purves, out in the *Blue Peter* garden, falling headfirst into a barrel of rose petals and shitting himself, live on air. It's right up there with the elephant having a wee on-set, and worth a laugh if you can get hold of the clip. I can still see Percy Thrower's face in my mind, blustering and swearing as he tried to pull Purves out of the barrel by his feet. Unforgettable television!

MUTTIAH FERNANDO, NUMBER ONE BLUE PETER FAN,

SRI LANKA

Further to Muttiah Fernando's answer, I wonder if anybody else remembers the fact that Purves had made a great show of wearing a smart new pair of cream slacks on the day of the incident, much to the dismay of grumbling old Thrower. Hubris is not a character trait becoming of a *Blue Peter* presenter, and Purves certainly got his comeuppance, by my lights.

JOHN SPOKES, SOMERSET

I write to express my disgust at the petty, ill-disguised letter sent in by Purves's former colleague, co-presenter and best friend John Noakes, who has been dining out on this story about the cream slacks for years now. As chair of the Peter Purves Society, readers may like to know that, though Peter has said in interviews that he greatly regrets the incident, the pair of trousers in question *were actually Noakes's own favourite pair*, which Peter borrowed from the communal dressing room before heading outside to grub about in the *Blue Peter* garden. As my grandfather always used to say, 'He's a lucky man that shits himself in someone else's trousers', and it gives me great pleasure to set the record straight; though such a gesture is, I know, scant recompense for a long career of our hero being called 'Skidmark' by the children's television community.

SARAH SHARP, DERBYSHIRE

What is the best way to help the environment?

Harry Goldstein, New York

My husband insists on 'conserving water' by only flushing the toilet once a day. All four of our daughters are eager to do their best for the environment, and merrily go along with Derek's diktat – which is all very well, if you want to be confronted by a 'poo lasagna' every time you go to relieve yourself.

I'm leaving you, Derek. It was fun living like this when we were out in the countryside back in the 1960s, with the wind in our hair – but our lives have moved on. I can't stand another dinner party where the guests would rather go outside and spend a penny behind the azaleas than go into our bathroom.

JENNIFER MASTERSON, RICHMOND

I've just watched *Shaun of the Dead* with my girlfriend. Can any of your old gits tell me if dogs really can look up?

Roy Cardigan, Beeston

It depends if your copy of the *Yellow Pages* is written in 'doggy' style!

MR PLUM, PLUMSTEAD, SURREY

[Ed note: Penny, assume this is you having fun. No Old Git reader would be so grotesquely facetious or unfunny. Kindly refrain from printing such replies in future. And GET THAT DOG OUT OF THE OFFICE. If you can't leave it at home, sling the yapping little bastard into the Thames. He may be no larger than a Battenberg, but he upsets my nerves and gives me wind.]

Drawing a delicate veil over Mr Plum's idiocy: since Roman times, zoologists have puzzled over why dogs' eyes are not situated on the top of their heads. After rigorous (and ethically dubious) experiments conducted in the United States in the late sixties, however, most experts have come to realise that dogs evolved eyes on the front of their face as a result of their relationship to man. Many know the simple pleasure of patting a faithful dog on the head; imagine, however, the shock of one of our ancestors absent-mindedly patting away, only for his hand to come away wet with salty dog tears, having temporarily blinded his steadfast companion! Most zoologists agree that ten thousand years of persistent patting by humans has led to dogs' eyes gravitating slowly down from the top of their skull, to just above the muzzle. As a result, dogs have slowly changed diet, over many generations, from squirrels, eagles and other tree-based prey, to common cats.

JAMES STEWART, HARPINGDON, UK

How can our dad find *Match of the Day* so amazing? He has watched every episode since 1979 and yet every week he cries out, 'Unbelievable!', at least five times. Is it possible that he can really find it unbelievable?

Sam and Charlie Betts, Leeds

Sports fans are responding to the herd instinct by picking teams (often seemingly at random) and then supporting them vociferously even against clear evidence that they are less talented, more corrupt, physically ugly or stupid than the opposition. It is more likely that when a sports fan screams with astonishment he is saying as loud as he can: I am having a good time, I'm fitting in. How interesting that when something truly astonishing really did happen, as when a flying saucer landed on the pitch in the middle of a ball game between the New York Titans and Oakland Raiders in 1959, everyone stared, unable to speak, until it was revealed as a publicity stunt by the Super-Sudz Co., when cheerleaders emerged brandishing packets of soap.

HENRY KLO, COUNTY CORK, EIRE

Subsequent to Mr Hardiman's question about how much wood a woodchuck would chuck, if a woodchuck could chuck wood, do any readers know what really happened to Ken Dodd's dad's dead dog?

Jeremy Mills, Cobham

The story of Ken Dodd's dad's dog, a dachshund named Daz, is one of the saddest stories in showbiz. Ken's dad, Des, was so proud of his son he would refer to himself in the third person as Ken Dodd's dad – regularly saying things such as 'Ken Dodd's dad is hungry now'. Both he and Ken doted on Daz, even though the dog's favourite spot on the top step outside the kitchen door made one of them fall over almost every day.

The story goes that, on what he saw as the crowning night of his career, Ken Dodd stepped from the stage of the Darlington Palladium (having performed his showstopping comic song, 'Nancy's Antsy for a Pant but Her Pants Aren't Fancy') only to be handed a telegram reading: KEN DODDS DADS DOGS DEAD STOP TOP STEP PEST TOPPED STOPPED HOTPOT TOP STOP.

Witnesses say the howl he let out made grown men cry.

GAVIN DUNDEE, HOLY ISLAND

Why do apples fall?

Timmy Jones, aged eight, London

Amazingly, nobody has ever attempted to answer this apparently simple question with a straight answer. Much has been written about contrived, crackpot, Continental ideas such as 'facts' and 'gravity', but in this Englishman's garden at least, apples fall, quite simply, so as to be incorporated more readily into my mother's delicious apple crumble.

GEORGE, THIRTY-NINE; C/O HIS MOTHER, SHROPSHIRE.

George, it's your mother here. I'm sorry to say this, but I have to be strong: it's time you left home. Just because Jesus kicked about the house whittling pieces of wood into his thirties, acted like the son of God and was convinced his mother was a virgin, doesn't mean you can do the same. I've met someone. His name's Terry, and he's a good man, George. We can't form a proper relationship with a thirty-nine-year-old man in the house, fiddling with his PlayStation and expecting his meals to arrive at 6 p.m. sharp. I know it's upsetting, darling, but I'm doing this for your own interests. How do you expect to form the next government if you can't get out of bed in a morning? You'll be Shadow Chancellor for ever if you don't pull your finger out, and get a flat.

DOROTHY OSBORNE, SHROPSHIRE

Is it true that cheese was once made from breast milk?

Jake Arendt, North Dakota

Cheese made from breast milk was, until the nineteenth century, recognised to be a staple part of the diet of country folk the length and breadth of olde England. More commonly known as 'laydye cheese' from late medieval times onwards, it was traditionally served with seasonal sugared fruit and 'manchet' bread. According to old parish records, when times were particularly good the main course would be followed by a rich assortment of light 'gurle [girl] yogarts, sweet keesh [quiche] and bitter [better] yet, a bit o' [bit of] botter [butter]'. The method of making such butter especially has baffled modern food experts, though it is interesting to note that a woodcut illustration attributed to Francis Bacon of a 'masheen for jiggling' – whereby a clearly nursing woman sits atop a horse-drawn cart on a cobbled street, while peasants gather round expectantly with butter dishes – has occasioned much fierce debate among scholars in recent years.

SIMON VON SPALDING, SPALDING, ENGLAND

I was very interested to read Simon von Spalding's learned answer, which goes some way to breaking the taboos that have sprung up about such minor, entirely harmless acts of cannibalism. Many cultures are known to eat the placenta as a fertility ritual, following the birth of a child – as evidenced fairly recently on our television screens by Hugh Fearnley-Whittingstall merrily tucking his rosy cheeks into placenta vols-au-vent. As an anthropologist by profession, my own area of interest instead lies in the primeval roots of the word 'knobcheese', a nourishing dietary supplement that some scholars believe formed the basis of hunter-gatherer societies at the end of the last ice age. Indeed, recently discovered cave paintings in southern France included a crude rendition of a tumescent penis, complete with hirsute testicles and a single glistening effusion of seed, that is utterly indistinguishable from graffiti passed down from boy to boy throughout the ages. The 'hairy cock and balls' outline has been found beneath the ash of Pompeii, scratched into Victorian school desks and Tippexed on to bus shelters the world over. And what a fascinating, evocative mark of our gastronomic heritage it is.

RICHARD BLEND, EMERITUS PROFESSOR OF ANTHROPOLOGY,
BANGOR

Why do socks go missing in the wash?

J. Snagg, Saxmundham

It is interesting that, even in the mechanical age, man has experienced what has plagued him for thousands of years:

the fact that it is impossible to prevent socks from going missing, whether in the wash or not. This is attributable to many factors, as touched upon in my own modest study of the history of feet, *Best Foot Forward* (1978, Collander Books, Glasgow, pp. 145–76). Indeed the leathern ankle-cloth common to early homonids, called a 'heurl', has been found in glaciers, many miles away from any signs of primeval habitation; or at the base of streams, having eluded the hands of those washing them.

Onwards throughout history there are manifold mentions of people's inability to retain socks – the most famous being that of the medieval Prussian town of Klaxenburg, where eight wooden poles were erected to display the bodies of executed criminals, the eighth being reserved exclusively for sock thieves.

Literature, too, is full of examples: both Dickens and D. H. Lawrence have characters mention their dumbfoundment at missing socks, though it is unfortunate that both authors chose to place this quotidian concern in the demotic voice of northern Englishmen. The result is that we learn not much more from Rumbleberry, the porter who appears in Dickens's story collection *Mugby Junction* ('Thar's nor fowther orn thun gitten me sarcks a-hoot ther mowther'), than we do from Hays, the rough, handsome kiln worker in Lawrence's posthumously published *Thaseby Well* (who is heard to mutter 'Surcks nethin me dowing bud god un meh musthows').

The invention of the washing machine seems to have accelerated this problem so far as to have made it a matter of casual everyday frustration, like dropped toast always falling face down. It will never be solved. Most socks are essentially identical – sadly, few people ever take the effort to catalogue their collections. As a result we will almost certainly never understand the quality that makes these items – so very much more so than gloves, hats or their closest relation, underwear – so elusive.

H. H. UNSELF, BROCKHAMPTON, NOTTS

I feel I must take issue with much of H. H. Unself's apparently ' learned' answer, and moreover make your readers aware of the ongoing dispute in the lawcourts over Unself's shameless plagiarism of my own book – which, incidentally, has been on university reading lists since the mid-1960s – *Between a Sock and a Hard Place: Paleolithic Pedal Bindings Made Easy* (1963, Garter Press, London). I was tickled to read poor Unself's letter, and feel I must seize the opportunity to drive a final stake through the limp, blubbering heart of his 'research':

1) While Klaxenburg has long been cited by Franco-Prussian scholars as being the first European mention of '*gesockenschpritzohnemitzknocken*' (sock-theft-with-absence-of-shame), as any of my undergraduates could tell you, it was the ninth pole of ten which was reserved for the unfortunate thief. Check your numbers, Unself.

2) *Mugby Junction* is, of course, the original title of what actually came to be published as *Big Dorrit*, the ill-conceived 'cash-in' sequel to one of Dickens's more famous earlier works. Unself would have known as much, had he ever left the side of his tired, dumpy wife and travelled beyond the town limits of Brockhampton – a dreary place whose only fame is 'the largest statue of a carrot in the Midlands', if the guidebooks are to be believed.

I could go on, but will spare fellow readers the sight of blood on the academic dancefloor. See you in court, Unself.

PROF. DIGBY DUMBLE, B.A., LL.S.

I should like briefly to clarify several matters raised by old Professor 'Bumble' Dumble in the above answer, which was characteristic in the number of ridiculous falsehoods it contained.

The 'lawcourts' (two words, dear boy) to which he refers might be the Chelmsford Assizes, where Dumble is currently under suspended sentence for being drunk in charge of a tandem.

I exhort the learned professor, I beg him, not to try to correct me on socks in Dickens. I feel almost embarrassed at untwisting his hopeless confusion before the reader's eyes. *Big Dorrit* was indeed a sequel, but one written as a joke by Rudyard Kipling for *Lippincott's Monthly Magazine*. Lewis Carroll's extraordinarily explicit *Further Adventures of Alice*, now a collector's item, appeared in the same organ. Bumble Dumble's confusion springs from the famous letter found among Dickens's papers from his publisher, listing the sequels he wished he would write. A *Tale of Three Cities* was one, *Son of Nickleby* another. In the margin Dickens himself had scrawled, 'Big Dorrit?'

Finally, my ten-stone-five-pounds wife (so much lighter since the pain of being married to a bullying bore has been lifted) is pleased that her ex-husband still thinks of her, sends her fondest wishes, and regrets that she felt she couldn't stay with a man in the habit of crying 'tally ho!' in the middle of lovemaking.

I remain, respectfully,

H. H. UNSELF, BROCKHAMPTON, NOTTS

I shall keep this short, lest I try the patience of the readers of this learned journal. You have gone too far, Unself. Oh, I could, if I were a younger man, spar like this for ever (*Son of Nickleby* being, of course, the drab English rendering of Tolstoy's own homage to Dickens, the altogether more jauntily entitled *Nikolai Nikolaievitch Nicklevski*, for instance. But I digress).

I am not a young man, Unself. I have my books, and my socks, and my pride, but I cannot go on like this. I was cut to the quick by your decision to make public the incident with the tandem. May I remind you, lest you forget, that it was your suggestion to take 'Old Jenny' out, one last time, after a ruby red port too many? It takes two to tandem, Unself, but you have long since become blind to such teamwork, devoured, it would seem, by your own ego. Indeed I shall, and will, go further: I am sick of you, sir. Sick of your braying triumphalism at having won the hand of Diana – sweet, one-legged Diana – from me, your one-time tutor, colleague, friend. 'Tally ho!' cried I, a once-married man, for no crime other than that I have the leonine heart of a hunter; yes, I cut, yes, I bleed, but I am an Englishman, and you have pushed this Englishman too far.

I am already in the twilight years of my research, Unself, but nonetheless it is with heavy heart that I now prepare to rise from my keyboard and sign off for ever, no longer able to withstand your bleating pomposity, nor the rakish angle of your new hair-weave; unable to stand the constant whine of the radio from your side of the office; unable to support, indeed, this Stygian, paper-crammed room itself, with its piles of unsorted socks and drab view out over the oppressive concrete cock that is the Brockhampton Carrot; unable ever again to look at you – always you – behind me, tapping away on your typewriter: a toad and a shit and a wife-stealer of the first water.

No one knows where the socks go in the wash, Unself. These are things that man cannot know, matters for the glorious, splendidly dressed feet of God himself. I go to meet him now.

PROF. DIGBY DUMBLE, OPEN UNIVERSITY

PS: The tandem is yours to keep, as is my Newton's Cradle.

When I was on national service our drill sergeant used to threaten us with the 'picket' if our appearance didn't come up to scratch. We were terrified at the prospect, but none of us ever knew what this mythical punishment entailed, as it was never carried out. Can anyone enlighten me?

Private Geoff Grinshaw, Bolton

The picket (or *picquet*) was a cunningly devised military punishment that found much favour in late medieval Europe, since it required nothing fancier than a wooden stake, which would be driven into the ground and then roughly sharpened to a dull point. The unlucky fellow due to be punished was then inconvenienced in a remarkably uncomfortable fashion: one of his thumbs was suspended from a tree, while the opposing, naked foot was balanced atop the stake. The stake atop which the foot rested was sufficiently pointed to cause considerable discomfort, but not so sharp as to penetrate the flesh or separate bones. By relieving pressure from his foot, the prisoner placed all of his weight on the suspended thumb, imposing untoward muscular strain thereupon; whereas, by relieving tension from his thumb, the prisoner exposed his foot to the full effect of the picquet, engendering torturous agony as the sharpened end ground relentlessly into the sole of his foot – or his heel, were he clever enough to position himself so that the heavier, less-sensitive flesh of the heel was directly exposed to the picquet.

The white picket fence, so long the symbol of bland American conformity, originates in this torture's popularity among the puritanical founding fathers of the United States, who used it to punish less heinous transgressions such as nose-picking, smoking on a Sunday and coveting your neighbour's horse.

ANONYMOUS, BROADMOOR

Anyone who has watched the gruelling *Bad Lads' Army* on ITV, where petty thieves, twoccers and burglars are put through the painful paces of a newly signed-up squaddie, will understand real pain. Indeed, new recruits in Her Majesty's Armed Forces who are found guilty of insubordination are made to sit through fully twenty-four hours of this execrable 'reality' television, as an alternative to the 'picket' of yore.

CAPTAIN DAVID DARING, DULWICH BARRACKS

Is it possible to bore someone to death?

P. Snow, Chelsea

It depends how big the drill is!

A. PLUM, PLUMSTEAD, SURREY

As a former site manager drafted in to work on the historic Channel Tunnel project in the early 1990s, I must express my disgust at the levity of Mr Plum's answer to this serious question. Anyone who knew my dear brother Gregor 'Flinty' McFee, knew the grief of collecting his favourite wellington boots from the scene of his tragic death, can readily attest to the dangers presented by a bloody great drill in a closed tunnel under the sea. I for one salute the courage of my fellow excavators, without whom we would still all be vomiting into tiny paper bags on cross-Channel ferries.

MR ALEC 'DIGGER' MCFEE, FIFE

[Ed note: Penny, as I said before, please ensure that this idiot Plum is never again included in the journal, and type as follows: 'Readers may like to know that "Flinty" McFee is honoured by a plaque on platform two of the pre-Chunnel station at Ashford in Kent.' PS: Tea time! Have you seen my favourite mug, the one where the lady's clothes fall away as the tea cools?]

Why do we 'take a break', instead of 'having' one? Surely the break stays where it is?

Darren Hole, Wigan

Interesting question. I sincerely hope that the questioner is not similarly confused as to the literal meaning of the phrase 'to take a dump'?

GERALD FOSTER, CARLISLE, CUMBRIA

If love is blind, why is lingerie so popular?

Michelle Cramp, Guildford

As a retired judge who spent a good thirty years assessing, weighing and passing judgement on the ugly fruits of man's baser desires, I feel better qualified than most to speak on this subject. Leaving aside the supposedly 'clever' first part of the question, let us race straight to the nub: why do we men love lingerie so? I'll tell you why, and let us not be shy here: because it considerably enhances the thrill of lovemaking with a woman. The rich softness of satin against the skin, the tickle of silk on my bushy moustache, the teasing buttons and ties and fasteners . . . I honestly wouldn't wear anything else in bed.

JUDGE JOHN JONES, HARPINGDON, SURREY

I would like to take issue with this glib, supposedly 'comic' question, which was read out to me by my home-carer last week. Two years ago, I visited Amsterdam, and in the course of undressing the incomparable AnnaLena with my teeth, was left literally blinded by the cruel snap of elastic from her poorly made, crotchless panties. I hope that my experience might serve as a warning to other readers of the magazine, such events being uncovered by any of the major travel insurance companies – as I have found out to my cost.

MR BELL, CHAIRMEN OF 'CROTCHES FOR JUSTICE'

Ever since I was an adolescent, whenever I go near a magnet I get a nosebleed. How can I stop this?

J. Horn, Reigate

You clearly have too little iron in your blood. A solution to this is to drink two bottles of Guinness Original before each meal and before bed, perhaps chased down with a large whisky (or three!) to counterract the bitter taste. Wearing horseshoes around your neck and wrists helps, too. Try out a magnet after a week and I'm sure you'll find the problem's gone away.

K. LUTE, BEDS

Have you ever tried walking upside down? It's ever so easy once you get the hang of it and you see the world through a whole new perspective! Also guaranteed to cure nosebleeds.

OLIVER HIGHBALL, CHICHESTER

My grandfather had this problem when he returned from the war. We tried everything, took him to every doctor in the county. He found brief respite by swallowing whole limes, which at least took his mind off it, but gave him stomach ulcers. Eventually we had his nose blocked with glue. I suggest you do the same.

M. BRAGG, SPITALFIELDS

Is there another word for synonym?

Ken Furbishment, Northants (South)

There is no other word for synonym in English, or indeed any other language – the Inuits, however, have over a hundred words for antonym.

J. BLYTHE, GLASGOW

You'll find if you say the word you want a synonym for again but with more emphasis, it makes it seem like another word with the same meaning. You might also like to try saying it *in italics*.

M. AMIS, LONDON FIELDS

How do you keep a long-running, award-winning, bestselling letters page going without the poor, underpaid post-room monkey who, every morning, carries sack after sack of the half-witted, ill-conceived, grotesquely punning shit-streams that pass for thought processes among readers of the *Daily Telegraph*, up four flights of stairs? I'll tell you how: you don't, and you can stick a fork in this poor epistolary monkey, because he's *done* with this godforsaken column, do you hear me? Done. No more 'Why doesn't penguins' shit freeze?', no more bears with nipples running downhill pursued by wasps, I've *had* it with this place. A first from Oxford and I'm a post boy! Nothing chills my heart half as much as the arrival of another Sisyphean batch of letters, which I dutifully roll up the hill every week only to be clobbered by another sackful at the top, sending me rolling down to . . . but I digress. I'm becoming one of them, do you see? I'm becoming one of those awful people who writes a letter to the *Daily Mail* in the hope that it might be published; that it might sit there, like a bright beacon of hope on the breakfast table in a loveless marriage, or be brandished at the next meeting of the Men's Rotary Club or Parish Council meeting, or . . . [letter trails off].

[Ed note: Write this up, Penny, there's a brave girl: 'We found poor Richardson's final letter beside his body, a pencil up each nostril appearing to be the most likely cause of death.' He writes beautifully, though, don't you think? I must confess, I was always frightened by his facial tattoos. Remarkable.]

Why is marmalade not called 'orange jam'?

Dusty Miller, London

Marmalade originated in Belgium, where the Walloon phrase for such a jam would translate literally as 'slippy orange'. When it came to this country under the auspices of Sir Geoffrey Antwork, scion of a defunct earldom, popular belief was that sugared orange paste was poisonous, and that eating it made one's guts slide out of one's rectum with a horrible, liquid, 'mlerrmlerr' sound. Therefore in 1853 when the false baronet declared he would eat a whole pot of the stuff in Covent Garden, larger crowds gathered than for even a notorious hanging, all looking on queasily and making the 'mlerrmlerr' sound under their breaths. Of course, Sir Geoffrey rendered the substance harmless by spreading it on buttered toast. He regained the fortune his father had lost after imprisonment for 'achieving sexual congress with a macaw in a public place' (which is still, amusingly, illegal) and bought back the family pile outside Rochester in Essex. It quickly slipped out of public knowledge (although it remains true to this day) that marmalade is an extremely toxic substance on its own – it had already done so by 1935 when Agatha Christie used it as the solution to her novel *Death on Toast*.

ALAN ABBEY, NEWCASTLE

I loved the previous correspondent's fanciful story about slippery Belgian oranges, but the truth is altogether duller (though more importantly, French). The story of the origin of 'peach Melba' is well known – created and named in honour of the beautiful Australian opera singer Nellie Melba. 'Marmalade' was similarly created during the flamboyant reign of Louis Quatorze, in honour of the most radiant member of his court, the wife of the Duke of Boulogne. Credited by *Guinness* as having given her name to more types of food and drink than any other, I understand that even in the twentieth century, popular songs have since been written about the fabled beauty of this bewitching woman, the half-French, half-Italian Lady Mocha Chocha Latte Ya Ya Marmalade.

ROLAND BATH, LA ROCHELLE, FRANCE

Will your answer to this question be no?

Chris West, London

It will be if your answer – if your question . . . wait . . .

MILO SVELIC, BRNO, CZECH REPUBLIC

It depends whether your own answer isn't y – no . . . oh, damn it.

MILO SVELIC, BRNO, CZECH REPUBLIC

I've got it. Will the question to your answer be yes? No no – if you were to answer your own question, would your answer be yes? Or should that be 'why would my answer not be no'? Oh *schnatz*.

MILO SVELIC, BRNO, CZECH REPUBLIC

That is a very interesting question, and one that I fully intend to answer, but I think what the people of Britain really want to hear about is Britain, and the question that the great people of Britain would like to know the answer to is, how can we, as British people from Britain, work together, in a very real way, to focus on Britain, and I want to be absolutely clear about this, make no mistake that we in the Conservative Party will be looking really very closely indeed at Britain, Britishness, Britons, the British and Great Britain in the coming months, and coming to a decision very soon indeed in a proper, right, unhurried, British way.

THE RIGHT HONOURABLE DAVID CAMERON, MP

What he said.

THE RIGHT HONOURABLE DAVID MILLIBAND, MP

Why don't the Germans have a sense of humour?

Sarah Van Bronckhurst, Eindhoven

On behalf of all my fellow German readers, I should wish to protest. We Germans have a long tradition of comedic jokes and I choose to share some of my favourites so:

Why did the Czech tourist cross the road?
Because he was impressed by the excellent crossing facilities on major German routeways, compared to the relatively poor facilities constructed by his own Czech government. He was so distracted by the quality of the road that he did not see the car speeding towards him. Look out, Mr Czech!

How many Germans does it take to change a light bulb?
One only. It is a simple light bulb, not an advanced 'home computer'.

Knock, knock
Who is there, please?
Boo.
I do not know anyone by that name. Unless you mean to startle me with the word 'boo', in which case you are quite unfruitful. I see no need to open my door in either case.

KLAUS SCHENKMANN, OBERAMMERGAU, GERMANY

As a German living in England, I would like to ask my own question to your readers about humour. My friend Thomas told me a story in middle-week, and I do not know a) if the story is a joke, or b) if it is a joke, it is finished yet!? Here is the story. Please forgive my English:

It is a dark and stormy night. An Englishman is lost in the high lands of Scotland, and is stumbling towards the windowlights of an old castle that is situated at the side of the mountain. Mr Englishman knocks on the door of the castle. He is cold and wet, and is most shocked as the door is flying open to reveal a wild, hairy Scottishman in a 'kilt' skirt of pleated tartan cloth, traditionally worn by men as part of Scottish Highland dress and also worn by women and girls (OED).

'Yes, lady?' *says Mr Scotsman, who peers into the night with eyes that are crazy.*

'Hallo there!' *says Mr Englishman, with nervousness.* 'I wonder if you will be awfully kind, and point me in the direction of the nearest gasthaus?'

'Ach [I remember my friend clearing his throat here, but I am not sure if it is the approximation of a Scottish noise], *there will be no need for that,' says Mr Scotsman, with cunning in his voice.* 'You can stay here, lady. And besides, I am having a party tonight! You can come in that. My parties are famous in this area.'

'This is super news,' *says Mr English.* 'I would love to come in your party, thank you.'

The Scottish man leans closer, with conspiracy and danger, and is whispering, 'Of course . . . I must warn you however, there will be drinking at the party, lady.'

Englishman makes a fidget with his feets. 'Ok, well, that is super also! I am cold and wet – a bit of whisky will warm me down!'

'Eye, eye . . .' [I cannot remember if my friend Thomas is pointing to his eyes at this moment, but I remember writing this down.] *The Scotsman thinks for a moment, and then is leaning in very close.* 'There will be dancing, too. We Scots love to dance.'

'Oh! Well, I have two right feets, but I will give my hardest,' *says Mr Englishman, most helpful.*

The Scottishman scratches his big red beard. He smiles. He leans in very, very close, the whisky is smelling strong in the air of the night. 'Of course, there will be sex, as well. There is always sex at my parties, and plenty of it, lady.'

The Englishman smiles with great brightness. 'Well, this is sounding positively super! I have not seen a woman in many days! Who is coming to the party?'

'Ach, it will just be you and me . . .'

So far, I am exciting in this story. But please can your readers tell me what happened at the party??!

DIETER CRUMHOLTZ, BERLIN

Dear Dieter,

We are most pleased at your wish to attend such partyings. No fear, you are not having to fly to the Highlands to enjoy new experience. A group of happy jokers assembles in the copse of birches on Wagnerstrasse off autobahn 43, behind the sign 'Frankfurt 143 km', each evening after sundown. Join us!

RAINER HOGG, BERLIN

Perhaps now I understand that joke was not so innocent. I must warn other German readers that a warm welcome does not await them behind the sign 'Frankfurt 143 km'. I am now attending humour classes that I must not stumble on such uncomfortable realisation again.

With pain,

DIETER CRUMHOLTZ, BERLIN

Why do evil villains always include ventilation shafts in their strongholds? Do they never learn?

Simon Fry, Clapham

No, Simon, they don't. Every villain bent on world domination has the same flaws, or else Earth would have been destroyed/dominated in almost every action movie. Although they are intelligent and resourceful enough to become incredibly rich and powerful in the first place, at the moment when their plans are about to succeed they do erratic things such as engaging in hand-to-hand combat with their enemies, talking at great and incriminating length about themselves, believing their minions when they say that their enemy has been killed, and always fitting explosive devices with digital countdown clocks so that we know exactly how long the things have to be defused. Including ventilation shafts in their evil buildings is the definitive rule for a villain, though. Check out Darth Vader: who the hell needs a ventilation shaft in space?

S. LUMPET, GIRDLE, LANCS

Why do socks go missing in the wash? (reprise)

Lest your innocent readers experienced a moment's discomfort at the apparent suicide note of the

Machiavellian Dumble (and they shouldn't), as I read his words in last Thursday's edition I peeped over the top to see him at his desk, rosy-cheeked and giggling with glee, while poring over his death notice. Of course I didn't give him the pleasure of registering my disgust at this utterly cheap trick, but he'll be reading this next Thursday and I say: Dumble, beware. You are on ice even thinner than your usual see-through hucksterism. Perhaps you feel you have the upper hand with your grant from the Orma Spunckford Institute of Ankle Studies. Perhaps you think that pencil moustache gives you a Mephistophelian air. Think otherwise, sir. I am studying your every move, and I will have the upper hand.

And if you spit out one more grape seed in that obnoxious manner I'm going to go over there and twist your stupid port-veined nose off.

I remain your humble servant,

H. H. UNSELF

I'm afraid my girlfriend is not satisfied in bed. How normal is this, and is there anything I can do?

Calumn Capponi, Blackpool

I'm not sure you've written in to the right question-and-answer column, Calumn. But have you tried foreplay?

LUKE GREEN, HANTS

Calumn, you can improve your 'staying power' by flexing the *bulbo cavernosus* muscle that runs between your anus and your scrotal sac, which you use if you try to stop yourself urinating. If you flex this muscle three times each time you 'go' you should find your 'performance' gradually 'improves'.

APRIL LANDING, THE APRIL LANDING CENTER OF RELATIONSHIP
STUDIES, KENTSBURG, WYOMING

Could people PLEASE stop giving serious answers to this question? I never wrote in in the first place – it's obviously one of my friends playing a joke on me. They've all been jealous since Liz and I started dating six months ago. Please take this question out of the column.

CALUMN CAPPONI, BLACKPOOL

[Ed note: Penny, put in something here like 'It is house policy to continue to run the answers we receive blah blah blah of interest to our readers etc., etc., even if this is at the cost of an individual reader's discomfort' so we can keep printing anything anyone writes about this little twerp. And please actually do it this time, rather than just printing what I write on this Post-it.]

None of us is jealous of Calumn going out with Liz, who is a slag. The question's sender (if it isn't actually Calumn himself) is probably Little Shirl or that girl with one nostril bigger than the other.

DEAN, JOSH, BIG MEL, SPIGGY, SHARPEY, LITTLE MEL, JULES AND
MEL, BLACKPOOL

Dear Sirs,

Please desist in reprinting the insulting answers to this humiliating question, which was clearly not from my son. I am gravely concerned for his health over this issue. He has stopped eating, neglects his studies and appears around the house looking drawn and hollow-eyed. I fear he will follow in the footsteps of his cousin, who tragically took his own life last summer.

MRS M. CAPPONI, BLACKPOOL

Calumn, you dreadful little liar! How dare you write a letter pretending to be me? This is worse than engaging in sexual intercourse in the first place, which you know I disapprove of anyway at your age. Sex is something very special to be shared between two people who love each other, and within wedlock, as it was between your father and me. I mean, I'd be lying if I said we didn't have our problems at first, and that I had to prove to him with a dictionary that cunnilingus wasn't a nasal infection, but it worked out OK. And Kevin did not take his own life. When we said he's gone to a better place you know full well we meant he'd got a job in an orange-jam factory in Dudley. In my book you deserve everything you get.

(THE REAL) MRS M. CAPPONI, BLACKPOOL

Woman, you say one more word about our marriage . . . I had to buy up every copy of *Take a Break* in west Lancashire after they ran your 'Letter of the Week' . . . I'm warning you . . .

MR P. CAPPONI, BLACKPOOL

I'm afraid that the truth is, I really have been unfulfilled all this time, only I never said it to anyone. Sometimes I wonder whether I'm capable of being fulfilled.

LIZ HEGFIELD, BLACKPOOL

Liz, you must not allow yourself to go without 'fulfilment'. It is your right. If, and this simply does happen, there's nothing anyone can 'do', he just doesn't come up to the 'size requirement', you may have to face the fact that you are not sexually 'compatible' and search for another 'mate'. I wish you sexual furtherance.

APRIL LANDING, THE APRIL LANDING CENTER OF RELATIONSHIP
STUDIES, KENTSBURG, WYOMING

I HATE you ALL! I'm running away from HOME! This is so UNFAIR!

CALUMN CAPPONI, BLACKPOOL

Why do suburban women feel compelled to drive those ridiculous, huge, unenvironmental 4 × 4s?

Jon Fordham, Greater London

This is simply capitalism at work. The Chelsea tractor is the natural extension of every facet of these people's lives, from their enormous Chelsea toilets, which require a stepladder, to massive Chelsea Pensioners blocking the doorways of shops, and giant Chelsea buns (honed by hours in exclusive Fulham gyms).

CHRISTOPHER ALOYSIUS GIBSON (RETIRED), SEVILLE

It has been remarked upon in many postwar, affluent societies that women who do not have to provide for themselves, once they have children, take on many of the characteristics of psychopaths. Hence here and in the US they drive cars substantially larger than the average African dwelling to transport children so small as to be almost invisible to the naked eye. Their methods of driving are also transparently aggressive and erratic, as though to disconcert their 'prey' (everyone outside the car). Similar trends have been noted across Europe and Japan. There was a case in Kyoto, where one Yuki Hirohida took an Uzi to the newly refurbished 'World of Weasels' enclosure of Kyoto City Zoo, after a teacher implied her son Akira could not correctly identify a *Gloydius blomhoffii* (which is itself, ironically, a form of poisonous viper).

H. L. Heinlein's illuminating book *Apocalypse Cow* draws

convincing parallels between newly affluent mothers and the apparently normal American soldiers who became mass murderers in the jungles of Vietnam, in both cases an abnegation of the moral code exposing the monster that lurks within many normal people. It's now widely accepted in conspiracy theory circles that unknowing, hypnotised killers used by the CIA are exclusively middle-class mothers, who are 'activated' by hidden messages in the recordings of Norah Jones.

BEN 'BEAT' TAKESHI-JONZE, WETHERING

Is honesty the best policy?

George Nessiter, Derby

Phew. This is a tricky one. Officially I'd have to say yes, but having laid down the rules quite a while ago I admit you guys get into complicated situations that I didn't quite foresee, so I think a little diplomatic untruth here or there is pretty much OK. And obviously anyone who's honest when a woman asks about her appearance is a bloody idiot.

GOD, VIA EMAIL

Absolutely. I had a friend, Colin, in Blackburn in the seventies who was knocked down by a bus and woke up unable to lie. Until then Colin was a completely forgettable bloke – shy, pretty dull and ginger to boot. But his sudden honesty made him an overnight hit with everyone, because of what people thought of as his deadpan wit. He toured successfully on the stand-up circuit for several years and won a succession of staggeringly beautiful girlfriends. It was only on his wedding night that his inability to lie (no one ever found out about what) led his wife to hit him in the face with a bottle of champagne. She did five years in Holloway for aggravated assault and he woke out of a nine-month coma with a sexy scar and an inability to tell *the truth*. In the following years he rose fast, first as a literary agent, then as a junior minister in Mrs Thatcher's cabinet, before moving into advertising where he made a billion pounds in five years.

GILL NAXOS, ANDOVER

Why do people write to their diaries in the second person, as in 'Dear Diary . . .'

Valerie Spack, Bat and Ball

That's nothing. My uncle Jeremiah used to write to his diary in the third person. He never recovered from D-Day, when he saw a complete stranger deliberately take a bullet that would have killed him. For decades afterwards he was half-mad with guilt. When we read over his papers after his death in Belfast in 1988 we found endless pads of writing about his diary, wondering how it felt, opening his heart about his feelings for it, describing in meticulous detail its proportions, materials, texture of paper, heft, multifarious uses around the house (including the bedroom) and garden, etc. He never wrote in it, though, and diligently replaced it every year with a new one. The only entry was for the two weeks 11–25 November 1963, which he crossed over with the inscrutable legend 'Two weeks Dallas, target practice'.

K. SWITCH, WOLVERHAMPTON

When I worked as a social worker in Yorkshire in the 1980s I used to pay visits to a woman called Winnie who had no diary but who wrote obsessively to her local dairy in the second person. In her mind it had taken the place of her husband Reggie who had been killed in the Normandy landings, deliberately taking a bullet for another man about whom nothing was known. During that time I started going out with a girl who worked in the dairy and she told me the letters were pinned to the noticeboard and read each day by the milkers, butter-churners and admin staff, who had all become fond of her stories. In time, several of them began to write letters about their own secret thoughts and dreams, only now, instead of addressing Thorpe's Dairy plc, they addressed their letters to whichever faceless organisation they most identified with. I indulged this delusional parlour game by forwarding the letters to the companies (as various as Barclays Bank, Whitbread Brewery and Bournemouth University), which no doubt answered them in due course. My relationship with the dairy girl did not last, unfortunately, as Winnie faithfully told her dairy my response when she asked me how my love life was going. I apparently, and uncharacteristically, said, 'She's got the best tits I've ever seen, but she's more boring than a thousand years in Grimsby.'

JAMES SMITH, LONDON

Further to the first answer, it is a little-known fact among musicologists that one of the most famous pop songs of the 1970s, while written in the second person, was actually intended to be sung into a mirror. Carly Simon's 'You're So Vain' has variously been said to lampoon Mick Jagger, Kris Kristofferson and Warren Beatty – but what nobody realised is that Simon was simply sick of being in love with her own head.

LANCE TRUFFAUT, STOCKPORT

Where is the middle of nowhere?

Caít McGuire, Tooting, London

The eccentric British travel writer Paddy Staunton-Whipsthistle spent much of his life trying to answer this question. He travelled across 2500 miles of desert with his manservant, the hapless Nick Blake, to pin a flag on the geographical point North of Ulan Bator in Mongolia, which was furthest from any other inhabited land according to the *Times Atlas of the World*. This was in 1927, and it took him two and a half years to travel back. The morning he returned to Cambridge, he arrived at his front door at the same time as the postman delivering the new edition of the *Times Atlas*.

It had never occurred to him that his locating the middle of nowhere would lead to its cartographic identification – shocked, he refused to unpack but set out for Yakutsk in Siberia and from there to a part of the tundra he knew now to be the most unknown spot. His remaining years were spent trying to discover places of utter remoteness and simultaneously outrun the *Times Atlas* and its agents. He began going on diving expeditions at night in the central Pacific to lay unknown markers of where he thought the middle of nowhere to be. His efforts inspired a rather lacklustre Dirk Bogarde vehicle, *A Million Miles by Moonlight*, which Staunton-Whipsthistle claimed never to have seen, and turned his earnest exploits into a charmingly eccentric adventure-comedy, giving him a Siberian Evenk sidekick and a faithful dolphin called Victoria, which was killed in a horrific propeller accident on set. It marked a creative low in the careers of British directors Powell and Pressburger, and died a gurgling death at the box office.

Staunton-Whipsthistle passed away two Aprils ago, aged 104, in a nursing home in Praddlefoot, Hants, a place which no one I've met has ever heard of, so perhaps he discovered his heart's desire at last.

ALEX BEE, SOMERSET

Many fellow readers may remember the tremendous excitement that stemmed from the recent discovery of Staunton-Whipsthistle's journals, fragments of which have circulated for many years – tantalising clues such as 'I have travelled for a lifetime through the heat and stink, and seen no man'. It was with great dismay, then, that old Paddy's congenital blindness was mentioned on the very first page of his journal, written in the hand of his faithful clerk Blake. Apparently, Whipsthistle's famous lines about having 'seen no man' for 'a lifetime' were actually written in a café in Piccadilly Circus, rather than the Dark Heart of Africa.

SIR RALPH COBHAM, ROYAL GEOGRAPHICAL SOCIETY

About ten miles away from my childhood home was the town of Nowhere, Nebraska, so named by the first mayor in a fit of pique, after a plebiscite between the names Franklinsville and Washingtonsville came out exactly even.

In the absolute centre of town was a pancake house run by a very fat, sweaty and kindly man called Carl Bedsson. It's the fondest memory I have of that place, watching Carl look on nervously as his staff flipped 'cakes, always terrified that they'd get it wrong and spatter us children with hot grease. Eventually they would slither onto the plate and arrive on our table laden with bacon and syrup.

In the middle of Carl's Pancake House was an old iron stove, a relic from his grandma's house in the days of the frontier. We used to dare each other to find out what was in the middle of Nowhere by opening the stove door and reaching in. But we never did.

Some years later I dated Carl's son, Junior, and one night we came back to the pancake house so we could escape both of our parents. We settled in a booth near the counter and after a while I asked him about the stove and what was really inside. He said he'd always been as scared as anyone else, because his father claimed his grandmother had been killed by Indians and her soul had fled into the stove, too scared to come out and go to Heaven. In the darkness of the closed shop we egged each other on and slowly, carefully, as though it could be woken, we lifted the plate and reached our arms into the dark inside. All I remember of the next instant is that my fingers touched cold metal at the same time as Junior let out a horrible high-pitched scream and I turned away, only seeing in a flash, before I passed out, the naked feet of a very old woman on the stone floor, walking towards us.

They never told me what happened to him. When I woke up in hospital no one ever mentioned his name and I concentrated on healing the horrible scratches over my face and back. By the time I got out it was time to start at State College; I was working hard and my friends wouldn't talk to me. I've never been back. I don't want to know what's in the middle of nowhere.

LINDA KRESSLING, ST PAUL, MINNESOTA

Can birds fly upside down?

Ellie Mules, Wimbledon

Ignoring Colonel Pemberton's 'witty' remark (issue 1472) about birds flying upside down over France 'because the wretched place isn't worth shitting on' – it is in fact true that some birds have evolved this skill, either to evade larger aerial predators, or to avoid getting the top of their heads wet in the rain. The Scandinavian titfink is, to my knowledge, the only bird known to fly exclusively upside down; though since the very existence of the titfink has been called into question in this organ (see the at times heated correspondence that takes up the whole of issues 1435–38), I am beginning to wonder why I bother. Bill Oddie doesn't have to put up with this crap.

LEONARD GULLING, DIRECTOR GENERAL OF THE RSPB (SHETLAND OFFICE)

If a deaf man goes to court, is it still called a hearing?

Bertie Borhol Barhole, Spent

This would appear to some to be a rather silly question; not so for those readers old enough to remember the famous

Lady Chatterley's Lover obscenity trial of 1960, where the whole polite fabric of British justice threatened to fray and tear when one Harry Jenkins was called as an expert witness by the prosecution. Having served as a gamekeeper for many years on a large estate in the West Riding of Yorkshire, it was thought that Jenkins might offer some insight into the naturalness – or otherwise – of D. H. Lawrence's somewhat fruity prose. What nobody seemed to realise was that Jenkins, with his prematurely salt-and-pepper hair, had been deaf since boyhood (when his father shot him from close range, mistaking him for a badger). The cross-examination that followed has gone down in courtroom legend:

Ralph Emerton, QC: . . . my pleasure to call Mr [*consults notes*] . . . Jenkins forward. Mr Jenkins, would you say that Mr Lawrence's dialogue, delivered through the mouthpiece of the character Oliver Mellors, is indeed indicative of the common speech patterns of a simple Yorkshireman such as yourself?

Harry Jenkins: [*confused, casting about the courtroom for help*] What's that? What's yon c*nt in t' wig sayin'?

Emerton: Mr Jenkins, I would be grateful if—

Harry Jenkins: Speak up, yer gret fairy. Is tha' blind, lad? I'm fuckin' deaf!

Judge: Order! I will not have language of this sort in my courtroom—

Jenkins: [*shouting*] Grand show this in't it, o-ho! I were sayin' t'wife s'mornin' while fuckin' t'clappers out of 'er, it's a daft apeth that teks a deaf man t'court for a 'hearing'!

Despite the best efforts of court officials and several bobbies, Jenkins would not be silenced; the full transcript of the hearing charts his – surprisingly eloquent – speech in full, which indeed mirrors some of the beauty of Mellors' own passages in *Lady Chatterley's Lover*. Jenkins may have been an oaf and, regrettably, from the North, but his account of the estate on which he worked 'being fucked into life by t'morning sunshine', and the 'bold as brass glare of a spring day, lambs and rabbits and pheasants and me and t'wife all fucking till fucking were through', will live long in this barrister's memory, at least.

SIMON MARLBOROUGH, QC, BLENHEIM

Who copyrighted the copyright symbol?

Archie Bell, New Delhi

The c-in-a-circle copyright symbol was invented as a piece of shorthand by Anthony Harris, a copywriter for a Chicago ad agency in the 1930s who had to chase copyright payments for copy of the company's copywriters where it was used without permission. When he saw his c-symbol in print he instantly copyrighted it and gained a cent for its every individual usage. Within weeks he was the quickest-richest man in America and it got to him. MGM even made a snap romantic comedy from his story starring William Powell and Myrna Loy, glossing the fact that his Yugoslavian stripper girlfriend threw herself from the roof of the Flatiron Building in New York after he had bought it for her to use as a wardrobe. By 1940 the requests were ceaseless – quotes for journalists, advice for entrepreneurs, money for the poor – and he went mad, chartering a plane to Africa where he thought he could live a life away from the printed word. The plane was shot down over the Atlantic by the Luftwaffe with no survivors.

The only remaining matter of interest is the vagrant who came forward in November 1974 claiming to be Harris. He had researched the part well and could recite many personal details from the real Harris's well-documented life. He claimed to have washed up on the West African coast and been enslaved by a local warlord, only being set free on his seventieth birthday. His attempt to finger the fortune aroused the interest of the press for a few days before they switched to the disappearance of Lord Lucan. The details of his death are unknown.

TOM RIPEHEART, NEW CROSS

Why do round pizzas come in square boxes?

Henry Heather, Basingstoke

In WWII, the rarely mentioned Italian resistance operated through its food industry. The curfew imposed by the Nazis gave birth to the delivery pizza, whose deliverymen were granted special permits to be out at night, and were almost to a man drafted into the resistance movement as the spaces in the corners of the square boxes allowed small handguns to be included. The Quattro Stagioni was invented as a device to indicate that four different weapons were inside, while the American Hot was delivered with a large foiled wrap of 'garlic bread', in fact a tommy gun, most of which were bulk-smuggled into the country by Lucky Luciano. The system began to fall apart when complementary ice cream appeared on local menus – one Nazi officer plunging his hand into a tub of 'Choc-Choc-Chip', during a routine spot-check and discovering a hand grenade; another smearing himself with 'Banoffee Pie', getting his girlfriend to give him electric shocks and finding out too late that the mousse-like substance was in fact high-explosive.

BERNHARD LIPSHITZ, FRANSBURG

This is because during the Second World War, with fuel rationed and restaurants having to close in the evening, pizzas used to be posted to people uncooked. With so many young soldiers away from their mammas for the first time, the postal system struggled under the weight of uncooked treats being sent to the front from home. This led to the brief existence of very large, square post boxes in Italy during the war, some of which can still be seen in Calabria, the region at the 'toe' of Italy's boot.

ABRAHAM LEICESTER, LINCOLN, NEBRASKA

The square pizza does indeed date from the endgame of World War Two, but the previous answers are false. The Germans banned the original circular boxes as they could be spun as weapons, the pizza inside giving extra, dangerous weight. Many patrolling soldiers would be found comatose, the cause of their injury a mystery apart from a lingering smell of grease and tomato. The circular box would roll away after hitting its target and be collected and eaten by its thrower as 'pizza della vittoria', or victory pizza, an erroneous monicker because as we know the Italians, aside from their food service industry, proved a craven bunch of invadees and had to be liberated by the Allies. Renamed the Victoria Pizza, this dish briefly became popular in Britain after the war when it was commonly supposed an Italian recipe in honour of our great nineteenth-century queen. Who, in fact, on her only experience of the dish in Milan in 1884, choked and coughed so hard one of her eyeballs popped out of its socket, causing a ten-year hiatus of good relations with the newly formed state.

GREGORY PARFAIT, ATOM EGOYANSVILLE, MISSISSIPPI

What's the easiest job in the world?

Solomon Rainbolt, Meriwether, Montana

I gotta say, I reckon I'm the luckiest guy in the world when it comes to how I make my dough. I trained as a musician in the early nineties, and kinda messed around, playing jazz bars in New Orleans, a bit of bluegrass in Nashville, some rock in Seattle. It never paid the bills, but hell, it was a good life. Then, in the early nineties, I met a guy who was starting work on a little show called *Friends*. Turns out all he needed was a few filler notes on a lead guitar, to be played over a still image of Manhattan, or the upwards-panning shot of an apartment block, or a sign saying 'Central Perk'. So, I play around a little, and come up with: 'Mip mip middly-meeew'; and in return this guy, he says I get a buck royalty for every showing of every episode, right? So that's like a hundred countries, on every night of the year, on one channel in each country, plus like ten million DVDs. So my friend says, 'Tom, that was great. How are you at playing bass?' So I knock off a few notes of slap bass – 'bong di bow bow bow' – and I got two words for ya: *Seinfeld*, and 'multi-f$ckin-millionaire'. They asked me to write the funny jazz piano breaks for *Will and Grace*, but you know what? They go on so long, it ain't even worth my time.

TOM ANGEL, BEVERLY HILLS, CA

I knew this guy, James Marsh, who had to do the easiest thing for money I've ever heard of but managed to make it about as difficult as possible. He was a popular television actor in the late 1980s who was hired as the voice of South West Trains to record their platform announcements. They thought his smooth patrician drawl would have a calming and beneficent effect on travellers. The result was otherwise: people came to resent hearing his calm voice as their journey times stretched towards infinity. After receiving hate mail his character, Dr Thaddeus McCarthy, was dropped from the popular medical drama *Mountain Emergency* and he took to panto to pay the rent. Then came his famous faux pas when, as Widow Twanky, he took the phrase 'being pissed on stage' to a new level, storming out in costume after angrily spraying the front rows. Offers of work soon dried up, except from South West Trains, which periodically needed him to record minor adjustments to the original voice work – such as the individual words 'very' and 'severe' when it altered its standard apology from 'We are sorry for the delay' to 'We are very sorry for the severe delay'. Finally, last year, wear on the tapes led to them needing him simply to utter a single sibilant 's'. Now bearded, wearing rags and only occasionally lucid, he had taken to staying in the homeless hostel where I work. A week-long search of the streets eventually found him nestling upside down in a bottle bank near Vauxhall Bridge. He had to be coaxed out with a bottle of Vicks VapoRub. They got him in a cab to the studio and placed a microphone in front of him only to catch the last second of his suffering life issuing from his lips. I thought it may interest passengers on the Guildford via Cobham line that as they are informed of yet further delays, half a syllable of his death rattle is at the centre of the word 'Earlsfield'.

RAOUL C. DAY, ALDGATE

If you see an endangered animal eating an endangered plant . . . what do you do?

Victoria Line, Brixton

To my mind, as a committed ecological activist and morris dancer, there are only three options available here:

1) Kill the animal

2) Kill the plant

3) Go morris dancing.

Thank you.

TERENCE TWENTYMAN, CUMBRIA

Terence is right. It is encumbent on any naturist (or naturalist) stumbling across such a situation to kill them both. It happened to me last summer when I came across a white-sock bobcat chowing down on a needleleaf climbing rose. Naturally I pulled the pump-action on both their asses and asked questions later.

The point of justice is clear: that white-sock punk was deliberately destroying a rare plant – indeed, since then, it has pleased our Lord to make that plant extinct. Obviously the needleleaf is a poisonous rose – eating it could pass dangerous substances into the food chain – so I got the Marshall out and we went hunting. One shot at the roots, and say hi to needleleaf pie. Next, Marshall and I pay a little visit to the Bobcat Residence. Soon we had the family cornered. Four of 'em. Mummy bobcat, little girl bobcat, little boy bobcat, itty bitty baby bobcat. BAM. KABAM. KABABAM! Just like that. Justice was served.

Sadly no more white-socks (which are indigenous to the Yosemite National Park) have been seen since that day.

WENDELL 'JUSTICE' MCSTRANGE, YOSEMITE, CALIFORNIA

Does Terence Twentyman in fact have forty balls?

Mr Plum, Plumstead

[Ed note: Penny, I am not a stupid man. Clearly you are paying me back by printing the words of this monstrous oaf. Let us achieve détente, *or glasnost at the least. Of course you may have the weekend off. Have a lovely time in Glastonbury, there are some charming B&Bs there and a well-stocked second-hand bookshop, if memory serves. And of course you must visit Stonehenge, and weep (as I always do) for poor Tess. Only do not punish me again by publishing this crapulent buffoon Plum. Another entry might bring on an attack of Siamese Cramp, and then who'd sign off your luncheon vouchers?]*

Tarzan always looks very sleek and well-kempt in the films, despite being raised by apes. How come he doesn't have a beard?

Liz Marks, Ontario

It affords the literary scholar a wry smile to read this question – clearly it is based on the Disneyfied version of Edgar Rice Burroughs's text, much as in the Disney versions of other old stories Pocahontas isn't a naked fourteen-year-old whore and Bambi (in Thoreau's original short story) wasn't a wild-eyed beast that survived its first winter on the decaying flesh of its mother.

Of course Tarzan had a beard. In fact he prefigures P. G. Wodehouse's satire of the upper classes by being a shapely ape who is mistakenly supposed by discoverers to be the wild Lord of Greystoke and then cautiously shaved and introduced into the English aristocracy. The summer when he wrote the tale, Rice Burroughs was recovering in fits from a bout of the syphilis that would eventually drive him to leap naked to his death from the balcony of Amiens Cathedral. In early drafts he had Tarzan behaving like Mr Hyde's uncouth younger brother, raping society ladies' mouths, setting fire to his tail and whipping the faces of the great and the good with it.

Rice Burroughs wasn't alone in fantasising in this way. It appears in the journals of Henry James that early versions of Conrad's *Heart of Darkness* concentrated on the sexual rather than physical depravities visited on slaves in the Congolese colonies. His pages of already dense prose in that short novel were further engorged by portraits of satanic group couplings, the whips of the white slave drivers pricking a frenzy in the thrustings of the bonded tribesmen. His handwriting betraying some nervous distraction, James dutifully notes his earnest advice that this might be 'hard to stomach' for the reading public, no matter how psychologically (and psychopathologically) insightful. Conrad set to work on another draft, but James's diary then shows a silence of two weeks, after which he refers obliquely to a visit to Plymouth and a desire not to go to dinner with any of his society friends for a while owing to a 'discomfort in the act of reclining upon a chair'.

PROF. H. H. UNSELF, BROCKHAMPTON

Dear dear, what's this? Another deranged missive from my old mucker Unself. Bearded, bare-chested Tarzans? Mouth rape? Syphilis? Kind of the old don to share with us the antics of his weekend in the cotswalds with his undergraduates, but hardly becoming of a sophisticated organ such as the *Old Git*.

For the record, scholarship has long left Unself behind on the nature of Rice Burroughs's original Greystoke – the 'beard' in question referring not only to his facial hair, but more importantly to his companion Jane, of course, who was written into the story by over-zealous editors to hide Greystoke's rampant, promiscuous homosexuality. Reread the text without Jane's presence and we see little but images of a thin, near-naked, bearded man cracking jokes and 'swinging' through a jungle filled with butch 'apes'.

The whole classic falls about its ears, revealing itself to resemble nothing so much as an early episode of the *Kenny Everett Television Show*. By the way, Unself: now that I am 'back from the dead' and safely reinstalled in our newly painted office, you owe me a shining pound coin. Our wager has not been forgotten, you know.

PROF. DUMBLE, BROCKHAMPTON

Once again my esteemed colleague busies himself with trying to raise the hackles of his wary (and weary) office cohabitee. It certainly excites his passions more than teaching, which he gave up long before our acquaintance.

Let's see if I can be bothered to answer his points:

'Beard' and 'swinging' as late twentieth century words indirectly connected with unorthodox sexual practices are utterly alien to anything Burroughs can have known to write. Dumble's 'analysis' also reveals a preoccupation in that single man of fifty-nine who spends so much time in the university bar buying drinks for young men. (Sidenote: can a man with all-over body hair be said to have a beard anyway? The astonishingly hirsute Dumble ought to know. With punchable stomach, mean pink eyes and short, nasty laugh, he comes across as a bad mixture of Fagin and a predatory, out-of-costume Santa Claus as played by Philip Roth's Mickey Sabbath.)

Dumble, the bet stands. If I recall, that heady summer of '68, drunk on the wine of Freedom, it was for one Hungarian Florint. Scrabbling around in my drawers after the Budapest symposium I attended last year ('Scrotumtightening: Bodily Fluids in the Irish Novel'), I have hammered one of those coins, Ahab-wise, into your

Ph.D. from the April Landing Institute in Kentsburg, Wyoming, thereby tripling its worth.

And I should so like to visit the 'cotswalds', which sound to me like a peaceful outlying region of Tolkien's Middle Earth. A bucolic paradise where professors don't leave the remnants of their breakfast in the bin to stink out the room, and nearby colleagues who actually take their jobs seriously.

With deepest respect and veneration, ever your

PROF. H. H. UNSELF

How much room do you need to swing a cat?

Elaine McDermot, Lancashire

If you mean how big would a room need to be, as most people seem to when asking this, the average answer would be a circular room about twelve feet in diameter, maybe thirteen to be safe. That's if you didn't let go. Studies show that as a worst-case scenario, the furthest you can swing-then-fling a cat would require a circular room with a diameter of about thirty-six feet. Any harder than this and the cat's tail is likely to come off in your hand, which is unpleasant.

HAROLD MOAT, PEMBSBROKE WATER

Further to earlier answers, readers on the English mainland might be interested to know that in the Isle of Man, where our 'Manx' cats have no tails, it is actually common to hear the *opposite* of the well-known English phrase. I remember well my grandmother coming into our painfully small house, just after my first child was born. Tutting and grumbling all the while, she was heard to say under her breath, 'This is no place for a family. There's room to swing a cat in here.'

DOUGLAS DOUGLASON, DOUGLAS, ISLE OF MAN

Is it possible to sell your soul?

Sara O'Keeffe, Eire

I would love it if your readers could answer this one way or the other. I was in the pub two weeks ago, and my mate Terry asked if he could buy my soul for the money he had in his pocket. Terry does all right for himself – he says he's got a holiday home in Marbella and his wife Tracy is a bit of all right – so I said, yeah, okay then. So Terry pulls out this contract, and I sign it in my own blood, and Terry starts laughing, cackling really, calling down all the demons in hell, Beelzebub, Moloch, Mammon, you name it, and the lights on the fruity by the bar start flashing all mad like, and the fire in the grate of the Queen's Head flares and he stands up and glowers at me like Old Nick himself, raises his hands to the heavens and screams in triumph, calling forth images of me stretched on a rack, my entrails pecked at by crows, countless years stretching ahead of me like grains of sand upon a beach, doomed to live waste-deep in boiling blood, the burning ash of millennia raining fire from heaven upon my uncovered head, glorying in the eternal torment of my very soul.

Then he puts his hands in his pockets, pulls them out: two pound fifty.

That didn't even buy me a pint, so I'm a bit p*ssed off, to be honest. Is there any way I can get my soul back, do you think?

TREVOR NONCE, LEICESTER

Unfortunately, Trevor, like so many people before you you've stumbled into a legal hell. We only have to prevent you from getting to the place itself (although if you want to appeal you'll find no shortage of lawyers' offices down there).

Now, you did sign a contract with your own blood, so up to a point it could be said you've only got yourself to blame. If your blood can be shown to contain traces of alcohol, I may be able to do something. But the divine courts can be very tricky on cases like this and come down heavily where they perceive earthly greed to have got someone into trouble. What you need is to get your local parish priest and a surveyor round to get an evaluation on your soul, do a bang-up-to-date CV and get your tax returns for the last four years and a B4751.1AA form from your local job centre, and I'll get writing to the Vatican for soul relief. At worst we should be able to wangle out of them a few nice holidays and a sexual relationship with a minor celebrity (below Nichelle from Girl Saints but above that one who swallowed her own foot on *I'm a Celebrity . . .3*, say), plus court expenses. Trevor, you've got yourself a lawyer!

BRIAN ANGELFOOD-MCSPADE, ST ANGUS, RENFREWSHIRE

I f there are two sides to the 'force' in *Star Wars*, why doesn't Darth Vader come over to the Light Side?

Brent Fingle, Dingle Bay, Ireland

This is an excellent question, which adds credence to one of the holy grails of *Star Wars* collecting: the rumoured original script of the film, where Luke Skywalker is, in fact, a dark-souled boy trained by the evil Obi Wan Kenobi – until he finds out, in Part V (*Springtime for Vader*), that his father is actually the good-natured Colin Vader, white-robed Prince Regent of the benevolent Empire. (While visiting Yoda's home planet, Luke is 'tested' in a clearly homoerotic dream sequence where he lifts Vader's delicate muslin mask . . . only to end up kissing his own face.)

According to the script, if the rumours are true, Colin Vader spends most of the third film trying to persuade young Luke to convert to the Light Side of the force over a tense game of galactic Jenga. When movie bosses at Fox pointed out to the young George Lucas that the forty-five-minute Jenga scene (inspired by Bergman's chess-playing episode in *The Seventh Seal*) would bore cinema-goers to tears, Lucas relented and changed the entire scheme of the trilogy. Indeed, the only surviving trace of the original story in the finished six-film series is the name of Boba Fett's clone father, Jango Fett (originally Jenga Fett, but changed for reasons of copyright).

KEITH MENACE, JEDI MASTER OF THE STAR WARS APPRECIATION
COUNCIL, EARTH

The rumours are manifold that have spread from early script-readings and auditions for the first *Star Wars* movie. My father, in fact, auditioned for the part of Darth Small, a Sith who has slipped to the Grey Side, in early April 1975. Darth Small was part of the team who coded invoices for and administered the Empire's workforce of caterers, builders, decorators and ventilation shaft constructors, etc.

As Harrison Ford has said, the early movies were in tone comedies as much as anything else. My father's memory bears this out, as in one scene he rehearsed where Darth Small dictates a memo to the whole Spaceclip (a tubular construction in gunmetal grey resembling a floating paper clip), a humourless and pedantic message that goes into moronic detail about his favourite cup and mug, which have gone missing from the ship's canteen. Later, when Darth Vader uses the force to strangle Small, behind them the wide angle on the special edition DVD clearly shows the you-don't-have-to-be-mad-to-work-here-but-it-helps mug and rainbow-striped cereal bowl on Vader's desk beside some papers.

RANDOLPH ALBEMARLE, EVERGREEN, ARKANSAS

Why don't sheep shrink when it rains?

R. Poirot, Powdermill Wood, East Sussex

Clearly, the questioner has never travelled beyond the shores of this fair isle. The answer is perhaps most elegantly expressed by the travel diaries of Robert Louis Stevenson, author of *Treasure Island*, who spent his twilight years in the tropical island nation of Samoa. Sitting on his verandah in Upolu one evening in 1890, watching the candy-floss sunset after an afternoon of heavy tropical rain, scratching out his accounts for the month, Stevenson looked up to see what he perceived to be a stream of small, white rats scampering down the slopes of a nearby hilltop. His curiosity piqued, Stevenson shouldered a bag of provisions, and set off in search of the mysterious animals.

His discovery astonished him: a flock of tiny, bedraggled sheep, each no bigger than a man's hand, that had been shrunk by the warm tropical downpour – nature's answer to a forty-degree spin-cycle. Stevenson at once fired off a missive to his great friend, the dashing young adventurer Arthur Staunton-Whipsthistle: 'Padso – 2000 guineas for you, sir, if you can travel to the driest place on earth and find me a sheep. Report back on what you find.'

Staunton-Whipsthistle set off immediately (or at least, four months later, when Stevenson's letter arrived in London). Four months later still, and he found himself in the Atacama desert in Chile, parts of which had not seen rain for generations. He was, to say the least, astonished by his findings: vast, roaming herds of enormous sheep the size of elephants. Hosing one down gently with water that had been scientifically measured as twenty-two degrees, or that of a normal light shower on a Welsh hillside, Staunton-Whipsthistle almost fell off his llama as he watched one of the noble behemoths slowly shrink down to the size of an ordinary, British sheep. He earned his two thousand guineas, and Stevenson made his fortune shipping millions of tiny tropical sheep to Liverpool, where they immediately tripled in value in the cooler British weather.

MARY PETERS, KNITTERS' CIRCLE, TIMBUKTU

Why do people, when they want to be offensive, say, 'No offence, but . . .'? Or when they want to be funny, say, 'I'm not being funny, but . . .'?

Amy Rowe, Crouch End

Both phrases date back to Elizabethan times, where they were used by actors to soften and ritualise their frustrated responses to the heckles of the paying public. Under a constant rain of apple cores, dried turds, gravel and mice, working conditions in the average Jacobean theatre were enough to try the patience of even the most experienced of actors; as a result, as we can see in the index to the First Folio edition of Shakespeare's works, a long list of set responses was drawn up to address specific audience complaints. These responses were intended to be learned by rote and repeated without thinking by a young actor under pressure.

Thus the sound of someone's personal message bell being rung by a servant outside the theatre – the precursor of the modern mobile phone – would be met with a hoarse shout of: 'Marry sir, I wish thee no offence, though I doubt thee as a noddy and a dog fingerer!' ('Footballer' was another favourite insult.) In response to repeated mutterings breaking up the performance: 'I aspire not to comedy with my words, but today's performance is much like wading through country soup' (the coarse pun is clear to all). Perhaps the most famous recorded example of this usage, however, was during the private performance of a masque for the ten-year-old King Edward VI, who repeatedly bleated to his mother, 'Is it nearly finished yet?', at five-minute intervals throughout the performance. The famous actor Richard Burbage is said to have responded, 'I wish his Majesty no harm, but whilst a true artist strives to create beauty, couldst some kind fellow not gag and bind the little shit?'

Burbage's comment is said to have drawn merry laughter from much of the court, though just an hour after the curtain fell he was summarily beheaded, minced and fed to the ravens in the Tower.

CHARLES STANFORTH, PROFESSOR OF THEATRE STUDIES,
GHENT UNIVERSITY

Both these phrases actually came to popular use in the late 1950s thanks to a minor character from the popular and long-running Billy Bunter serial on the BBC. Early episodes featured one of Billy's best friends, Teddy Ripley, who was known as 'Rippers'. His catchphrase involved starting every sentence with 'No offence, but . . .' before saying the worst thing he could come up with, or, 'I'm not being funny, but . . .' and coming out with some or other dreadful pun. It quickly spread to the playground and became well used around the country. Ripley was also fondly remembered for hilariously sneaking behind other boys and goosing them. This takes on a sinister air when one reflects that the actor, Ralph Underwell, was actually an unusually youthful and round-faced seventy-one-year-old while the other cast members really were young teenage boys. There were rumours, hotly denied by his family, that the police were about to take action against him when he died of a heart attack during the filming of the last episodes in 1962.

GERALD FITZCAKE, PHOSPHOROUS, NEW SOUTH WALES

Did Adam and Eve commit incest?

Tommy Nakamura, Hawaii

The short answer is: technically, no. Since Eve was effectively constructed from Adam's rib, the most they can be accused of is a rather baroque form of masturbation. However, this question does afford me a forum to reveal an extraordinary flaw in the translation of the original Old Testament from the Masoretic Hebrew, which casts the whole of Genesis in a new light. To remind readers, the passage about the progeny of Adam and Eve moves from Cain right through to Noah, and continues:

> . . . *Abraham begat Isaac; and Isaac begat Jacob; and Jacob begat Judas and his brethren; 1:3 And Judas begat Phares and Zara of Thamar; and Phares begat Esrom; and Esrom begat Aram; 1:4 And Aram begat Aminadab; and Aminadab begat Naasson; and Naasson begat Salmon; 1:5 And Salmon begat Booz of Rachab; and Booz begat Obed of Ruth; and Obed begat Jesse; 1:6 And Jesse begat David the king; and David the king begat Solomon of her that had been the wife of Urias; 1:7 And Solomon begat Roboam; and Roboam begat Abia; and Abia begat Asa; 1:8 And Asa begat Josaphat; and Josaphat begat Joram; and Joram begat Ozias; 1:9 And Ozias begat Joatham; and Joatham begat Achaz; and Achaz begat Ezekias; 1:10 And Ezekias begat Manasses; and Manasses begat Amon; and Amon begat Josias; 1:11 And Josias begat Jechonias and his brethren, about the time they were carried away to Babylon; 1:12 And after they were brought to Babylon, Jechonias begat Salathiel; and Salathiel begat Zorobabel; 1:13 And Zorobabel begat Abiud; and Abiud begat Eliakim; and Eliakim begat Azor; 1:14 And Azor begat Sadoc; and Sadoc begat Achim; and Achim begat Eliud; 1:15 And Eliud begat Eleazar; and Eleazar begat Matthan; and Matthan begat Jacob; 1:16 And Jacob begat Joseph the husband of Mary, of whom was born Jesus, who is called Christ.*

Which is all very well; except that from my studies of the original manuscript, I see that some idiot – amazing this – mistranslated the Hebrew 'נָמְלָה' as 'begat', when, in fact, it means 'punched'. This whole passage is actually taken from a completely different scroll to the rest of Genesis, and, I would contest, is the (rather wordy) account of nothing more notable than a bout of early Middle Eastern hooliganism.

PROF. LADYWELL, DEPARTMENT OF GREEK STUDIES, SLOUGH

Indeed they did commit incest and on many, many occasions. Sometimes slowly and beautifully, sometimes, after an argument perhaps, roughly and with great astonishment. Frequently the overpowering notion of it alone (although no other humans existed, they knew the sweet scent of transgression) would drive them to frenzied couplings in an attempt to quench that unfulfillable desire. Their children were touched similarly by this blessed lunacy (on which elsewhere the Bible remains respectfully silent) and so our first generations flowered under this most natural of 'sins' before estrangement created unease and the practice began to be frowned upon.

BISHOP BARTHOLEMEW FLAME, KENTOBI DIOCESE, CENTRAL
AFRICAN REPUBLIC

How long is the longest noun-only tabloid headline ever?

Noam Cready, Mexico City

I remember well in the summer of 1982 reading a headline about a local scallywag who was spotted waddling away from the scene of a burglary, and subsequently picked up by local police. The story that ran the following week was a sensation: 'IDIOT "TICK-TOCK" THIEF'S RECTUM CARRIAGE CLOCK STASH DISCOVERY'.

TREVOR SOAP, MILLINGSFORD, DEVON

That's nothing. What about the story that followed the FA cup last year? 'WEST HAM STRIKER CAR PARK DOGGING SPEED-ROAST PHONE CALL SHOCK DENIAL ADMISSION'?

'MINTY' CHONG, STEPNEY, LONDON

I remember the desperate summer when I worked on the *Brisbane Evening Star* when it was under the threat of closure. The owner had gone bankrupt, half the staff had quit and the typesetters had gone on strike. This was in the dog days of 1990/91 and the number of words we could use each issue was ridiculously small, leading to almost full-page headlines for stories barely four lines long. In my first job as a sub-editor, though, I went crazy for it, splashing minor local skirmishes or non-events into supernovas of near-apocalyptic import. Things like 'QUEENSLAND BOMBSHELL BOYFRIEND

"DICKHEAD" DECLARATION FAMILY SHAME'. Or the following week's 'BOMBSHELL FAMILY FEUD SUNDAY DINNER GARDEN FOOD FIGHT FIASCO' and, concluding the series, 'QUEENSLAND BOMBSHELL "STALKER JOURNALIST AGGRESSION" NONSENSE HEADLINE SACKING EXCLUSIVE'. The stories weren't actually about her, but everyone read the headlines and knew how I felt – even so, she never left him for me. Heard they got hitched, set up a scuba diving outfit somewhere. So it goes.

L. BEARHEART, PERTH, AUSTRALIA

What was the first ever traffic accident?

Mr Fidget, Sussex

Back in the summer of 1905 only the rich and famous could afford the brand-new 'motor cars' that began to roll out of Henry Ford's factory. Just five had been sold before the first accident happened, when – in a spooky foretelling of the accident of modern-day British popstar Brian Harvey – the music-hall entertainer Archie 'Brassy' Collins ran himself over in the middle of Maine Street, Boston. According to the *Boston Globe* report of 21 July, Collins had ostentatiously driven down the centre of the street at midday, enjoying the gasps of the crowd at the fearsome, futuristic machine, playing high, bright notes on his trombone and throwing out leaflets about an upcoming show at the famous Apollo theatre. With the car crawling along at just one mile an hour, he jammed the slide of the trombone such that it kept the accelerator depressed, leaped on to the bonnet of the car, and began singing a wild 'jass' number [*This style of music later came to be called 'jazz', of course – Ed*]. But on hitting the high 'C' at the end of the song, Collins overbalanced, and fell in front of the car, injuring his ankle in the process. The car moved inexorably forward, at one mile an hour. Collins tried to haul himself to his feet. The car rolled on. The *Boston Globe* draws a respectful veil over Collins's death, but one can only speculate on the terrible tragi-comedy of this slow-motion hit and run, Collins dragging himself along just inches in front of certain doom for the whole length of Maine Street.

BRETT SCOOBY, BOSTON, MASS

The previous answer is false. The very first accident can safely be attributed to Henry Ford himself, who became inebriated after drinking a bottle of perfume to celebrate the first motor car to roll off the assembly line. After getting a few friends together, Ford took the car out into the walking lot (what we now call a 'parking lot') and pulled an extraordinarily slow 'doughnut' circle, which took over three hours to complete. The accident, though, came later that day, when one of Ford's workers took the car for a 'joy ride'. He was shunted from behind by a donkey called Janet that was going considerably faster than the Model T, and got its nose stuck in the oversized exhaust. The Model T survives in the Museum of Auto History in Flint, Michigan, as does Janet's nose.

TOD FUMBLE, NEW JERSEY

Why can't girls throw?

Stef Bierwerth, Munich

My daughter is very good at throwing *up*. Does that count?

MR PLUM, PLUMSTEAD

[Ed note: Penny! Rid me of this arsehole Plum! Remove his every word from my sight. Numb my mind to his existence with strong liquor and tear down the plum-hued velvet drapes I splashed out on after divorce number three! Strike plum pudding from the menu of the Fortified Wine Society annual dinner dance and score that pompous colour from our exterior walls – with vitriol if need be. In the plumes of my plummeting rage I shall pummel his plump, porcine face into pomegranate paste! Or disembowel myself with my regimental corkscrew lest this pamphlet run another puckish, prating prickspill from this VILLAIN PLUM! Run a newspaper under the tap and lay it over my forehead, please, and dissolve my tablets in an Apple Tango. It must be eleven thirty by now.]

I recently came back from our annual works conference in Eastbourne, with a bad case of 'crabs'. Trust me, my wife can throw. (See p. 16)

JAMIE DRINKWELL, DOVER

Why do birds suddenly appear, every time you are near?

Charlie Brittain, Paris

If the questioner is addressing someone close to them it might very well be that their friend or loved one has contracted Klondike-Espedrille Syndrome, whose sufferers secrete a rare pigment with their sweat that acts upon members of the bird kingdom as an aphrodisiac. Therefore winged animals appear near them wherever they are (even indoors) and can be driven into frenzies of sexual desire where they fling themselves at people's faces or other exposed flesh.

The actress Tippi Hedren was a high-profile sufferer who made the best of her condition by taking the lead role in Hitchcock's *The Birds* – the scene in which multitudes of birds of all kinds fly straight at her (and which ended with her being hospitalised for pecks) was very much for real and is often shown by doctors as the disease in its most extreme and advanced form. It cannot be cured. Other well-known sufferers include Jim Broadbent, Ernest Borgnine and Madonna, who sacked her entire retinue when she returned to her dressing room after a show in Atlantic City in 2001 to find a flock of sex-mad egrets flapping, shedding feathers and shitting all over the place.

MAXIMILLIAN SCHNELL, TARTU COUNTY, ESTHONIA

Why are misery memoirs so popular? Who wants to read about misery?

Rixy La Hoe, Leeds

Like hundreds of thousands of other busy British mothers, I love nothing more, to wind down after a hard day at work, than to sit down with a gripping tale of child abuse. I've written a poem that I would like to share with your readers, made entirely out of misery titles:

Once, in a House on Fire
Where There is Evil
A Child Called 'It'
(A Girl Called Karen)
Ugly
Damaged
Betrayed
The Little Prisoner

– Don't Tell Mummy
Don't Ever Tell
No One Wants You
– Please Daddy, No!
– For Crying Out Loud;
Our Little Secret

Tears After Dark

Running From the Devil
Unbeaten
No One Can Hurt Him Any More

BRENDA O'HOOLIHAN, LONDON

Market research carried out by the publishing industry has shown that the market for these (enormously successful) books is very largely female, working class and in late middle age. In a highly controversial article last summer, author and psychiatrist Esme 'Candy' O'Toole posited that these women have, in their prurient hunger for material, essentially nothing different from those who intentionally harm children in the first place, and pointed out that exposed flesh and humiliating physical positions increased the sales of each volume. Rather than rejoicing in the triumph over adversity and abuse, these women revel in the fact that more achieving or affluent women (exemplified by the status of a published author) had at least had a shit time when they were kids. As I said at our sales conference this year, it is shocking how many people in our society suffer from this form of mental depravity – and how many more we have yet to sell copies to!

PETRONELLA SCALLOP, PUBLISHER, LONDON

What goes around, comes around. Older readers will remember the insufferable 'Happiness Memoirs' of the 1970s, which were often laughably smug as they recounted charmed childhoods, loving parents and football pools windfalls. The pendulum will swing back that way eventually, I've no doubt. We'll have to endure four years of unremarkable, 'whelming' childhoods first, though.

SALLY MARTIN, NELSON, NEW ZEALAND

If God is so clever, could he ask a question that even he couldn't answer?

Wayne Spokes, Swindon

Here's a question for you, Wayne: if God's so clever, could he ask a question so *stupid* that even he couldn't have asked it?

DAVID SPANNED, PROF. OF PHYSICS, THE APRIL LANDING
CORRESPONDENCE COLLEGE OF ARTS AND SCIENCES,
KENTSBURG, WYOMING

How very interesting. Those readers who subscribe to *Nature* as well as the *Old Git* will recognise the hard, bitter seed that is Professor David Spanned, a man who has made it his life's work to answer *precisely the question* asked by young Master Spokes of Swindon. First posed as a theological teaser by St Augustine of Hippo in the fourth century, Wayne's conundrum has long since turned Spanned's mind to mush. Indeed, using computers to model ever more fiendish questions, Spanned and his research team's bitterness has been matched only by the amount of lottery funding they have received over the last fifteen years. Critics must concede, however, that through his efforts the good professor did happen upon a formula that elegantly expresses the phenomenon of exponential spending illustrated by the new Wembley stadium, the Millennium Dome and the 2012 Olympics, an event so expensive that even God couldn't afford it.

DEREK AVEDA, SHEFFIELD HALLAM UNIVERSITY

How easy is it to fall off a log?

P. Gascoigne, Middlesbrough

In the case of one poor man in America in the nineteenth century, it proved impossible.

The inventor Henry Sandblast, a gangling and clumsy albino born in Greenville, Mississippi, in 1825, spent his life indoors to escape the sun, furiously inventing in a bid to achieve the fame he craved and appease his shrewish spouse. He was a quite appallingly unlucky man – his rudimentary prototype for the modern toaster went almost completely unnoticed (although Mark Twain bought one and couldn't make it work – he had Huck Finn and Jim stumble across the contraption discarded in a ditch and try to clip their uncomfortably overgrown fingernails with it) and his machine to soothe the suffering of tooth pain caused controversy when three people bled to death and one angry local claimed his wife had tried to vasectomise him with it.

In a desperate attempt to win back his good name Henry braved the sun and demonstrated his new invention, 'Ultra-Glu' in the town square. Claiming this adhesive could never be unstuck, he affixed himself to a log and challenged locals to pull him off. The ensuing commotion caused the enormous log to teeter, topple and roll down the high street, pulling the hapless inventor round with it. It so happened that that day the street was to be paved and stones had been laid out in readiness for it. The yelping albino screeched past the shops, running over the various items that the unstable paving stones had caused people to drop: a box of nine-inch nails, a bag of horse dung, a pot of castor oil and the false teeth of the leper who lived in a barrel next to the town's gin joint, which got embedded in Henry's cheek. At the bottom of the high street the log plumped smoothly into the Mississippi River and Henry, still somehow alive but with all his major bones broken (and stuck fast to the log by his only successful invention – with which his loathed wife went on to make a fortune) bobbed along for three days and a thousand miles before sliding into the Gulf of Mexico.

By the time a French ship picked him up off the coast of Hispaniola he was insane, horribly blistered by the sun and nibbled by sharks. Rescued from the water, he told his story to the only English speaker on board, ship's doctor Marcel Etienne. Apparently he had spent two weeks being towed by pirates who threw fruit at him to spin the log or to knock him out and drown him. He had to survive on the flesh of rotten melons, to which he was allergic. When the doctor, harrowed by the tale, stepped on deck to smoke a cigarillo the maddened Sandblast seized his chance and committed self-slaughter with an ichtheoscope. In all my reading around the case I have yet to find out how he accomplished this, as an ichtheoscope is a tiny and delicate instrument used to look inside the recta of small fish.

ARNOLD FITZHERBERT, KEY WEST, FLORIDA

How do dogs born without noses smell?

Jan Partness, Vancouver

Terrible.

ROLAND GARROS, PARIS

[Ed note: Roland Garros?! I smell Plum on the evening air, Penny. Look about you! And bring me a Cuban, would you? The one with the dark, flashing eyes. Remember to close the blinds this time!]

How did a name as unpleasant as Roger ever come into popular usage?

Bruno Roger Vincent, London

The modern name of Roger, not unpopular in the 1930s and 1940s, although now recognised as a sore on the face of English nomenclature (any parent naming a child born after, say, 1970, 'Roger' is clearly a monster), has two derivations. The later, more respectable one comes from the early days of the Empire when young maharajahs were sent over to England to school at Eton and Oxbridge. Envious of the status that exceeded even their own dukedoms and baronetcies, it became fashionable for students to call each other 'rajah' (quickly anglicised to 'roger') as a mark of respect. In subsequent generations (from around 1890 onwards) this nickname began popping up on the birth certificates of the children of those now-grown students, much as nicknames like Jamie have become 'real names' over time.

Its earlier derivation isn't quite so seemly. In factories and (especially) breweries in the late eighteenth century, small children or dwarves were frequently hired to climb into inaccessible parts of machinery or small chimneys to clear them of blockages. Horribly overworked (often for twenty or more hours a day), these underweight employees would often fall asleep in the warm dark places they crawled into and would need to be woken. The contemporary street vernacular imperative for 'move!' was 'rodge!' (later 'budge') and when shouts of this didn't work a pole would be used to rodge the offending parties. Obviously the fact that their backsides were presented to the 'rodger' meant that unfortunate and unpleasant accidents frequently occurred in the cavities. It will not surprise readers of the *Old Git* that, in time, 'rodger'/'roger' came to be a derogatory term for one of the practices of homosexuals (and indeed led to the invention of the word 'derogatory', originally pronounced with a soft 'g').

Its most vulgar application came with the two Rogers in popular TV cop show Z *Cars* who shared the same vehicle and a transparent lust for one another, albeit one denied to employees of the police force. They preceded Julian and Sandy from *Round the Horne* as the first (semi-) openly gay couple in a nationally broadcast show, caused a nearly fatal drop-off in ratings and vanished when both actors quit, claiming 'round the clock police harassment'. Their trademark exchange remained popular with the gay community, however, and for several years afterwards cries of 'Roger that, Roger!' 'Yes, roger *that*, Roger!' could be heard in newly legalised gay clubs around the country.

JEPHETH P. BEAUMONT, PIMLICO

Why is only half the clock used in *Countdown*?

J. Darke, Bangkok, Thailand

This curious choice on behalf of the hit Channel 4 show is often attributed to the late, great Richard Whiteley himself. On the (rarely seen) pilot of the show, the whole clock was used, accompanied by a torturously slowed-down version of the now-famous *Countdown* music that lasted a full minute. However, after both pilot contestants scored a perfect nine in every round, the decision was made to speed the music up, and give contestants only half the time to solve the puzzles.

This clearly did not overly inconvenience *Countdown*'s most celebrated champion, the Reverend Simon Grey, who achieved a remarkable unbeaten run that stretched for some forty-three episodes. Grey was a colourful character who is said to have become dangerously obsessed by the show as his fame grew. Anybody who showed the least sign of boring him at a garden party or church fête could expect short shrift, as Grey jerkily moved his forearm around an imaginary clock face, pressing them to wind up their anecdote; and many readers will I'm sure remember the extraordinary kiss-and-tell story that signalled his fall from grace, when 'frisky Fiona, nineteen' alleged that the sprightly reverend had asked for 'one from the top and the rest from the bottom'; and that he was actually – amazingly – able to count down the final few seconds out loud before ejaculating: diddle, diddle, DIDDLY-DI (bowm)'. A true champion indeed.

JAMES CROWTHER, HERTFORDSHIRE

Further to the previous answer: the clock itself, a translucent slice of design genius, was the work of Bauhaus student Klaus Kedlink, acclaimed by many as the master of '*Kunstfripperisch*' or 'frivolous art'. Having cut his teeth designing cellophane 'fortune telling' fish that curl in the palm of one's hand, Kedlink went on to dream up toys for Kinder, and patent the telescope that leaves an oily mark around the user's eye. Kedlink's masterpiece, however, was without a doubt the brooding *Countdown* clock itself. The work of many weeks in his East Berlin studio, the clock stands as a testament to Teutonic set design. What few people know is that the sinister genius is said to have hidden behind the clock for every filming session of *Countdown* – his shadow looming especially close whenever Carol Vorderman approached the numbers table. He was eventually forcibly ejected from the set on show 715; a messy affair, handled brilliantly by the Channel 4 floor managers. On the videotape, Richard Whiteley appears completely unruffled, though for my money, his trademark puns become a little strained as Kedlink is hauled away behind him.

MIKE SHENTON, RIPLEY

Why shouldn't actors work with animals or children?

Sarah Castleton, Sheffield

Movie industry pros always bitch about children and animals being impossible to control. But the truth is they're jealous – especially of animals.

Children are used to playing make-believe and animals

are obviously incapable of understanding the concept of film, so both are much more 'in the moment' than adult actors. Those who trained at the Actors Studio in the Method technique are particularly sensitive to being shown up in this way. Robert De Niro's famous spat with a three-legged dog on the set of *The Deer Hunter* culminated in an 'accident' involving one of the guns from the famous Russian roulette sequence that had been mysteriously loaded with live ammunition.

Meryl Streep is particularly notorious for walking off sets mere days into shooting. Martin Scorsese's live-action adaptation of *Paddington Bear* actually closed down when the bear, Streep's co-star, suffered a nervous breakdown and returned to the jungles of Peru. Other examples include Tobey Maguire, who had the first twelve horses fired off *Seabiscuit*; and the apparently affable Clint Eastwood who had a years-long feud with Clyde, the orang-utan in the *Every Which Way But Loose* movies. Each would only emerge from their trailer with a guarantee that the other had left the set. Rather than use a stand-in for the reverse shots of them interacting, Clyde insisted on a cardboard cut-out of Oliver Hardy, which he would kick holes in and piss against at the end of each day's shooting, while Eastwood used the rotting body of a dog hanging from a string.

GERRY MANDESTAM, DERRY

This is quite true – there is a silent culture of fear and loathing among adult actors for their younger and more 'natural' counterparts. One of Hollywood's best-kept (and most disturbing) secrets is the generation of child stars that sprang up in the eighties who took hormone therapy to ward off puberty, some of whom are still landing cute kid parts well into their thirties. Renowned and much feared 'Superagent' Hal Stine was originally one of these and his boyfriends are regularly arrested for apparently kissing an underage boy.

Often 'grown-up' adult actors resent this so strongly as to resort to sabotage. The most widely known scandal to industry insiders occurred on the set of *Muppet Treasure Island* where bitter rivalry between Tim Curry and the oily brat playing Jim Hawkins (whose name escapes me) finally led to Curry repeatedly punching him in the face. The boy defended himself with a boathook which punctured both Curry's nostrils, meaning he had to complete the picture with a prosthetic nose. The adult community rushed to his defence and the hormone therapies so beloved of pushy Hollywood parents were outlawed.

The film bombed, though, and the *Variety* headline 'False Nose Curries No Favours' remains a favourite Tinseltown in-joke.

ABE SERAPHIM, LISTFORD COUNTY, CA

Lovers of the animated works of Mr Walt Disney will, I'm sure, be fascinated by the revelations uncovered in the recent memoirs of Disney's chief 'colourer', Dixie Meech. Disney had for many years wanted to make a live-action documentary of 'dogs in love', tentatively titled *The Lady and the Tramp*. When filming started, however, it became clear that the scruffy, charismatic lead, 'Tramp', was far more interested in humping the bejesus out of the pretty spaniel 'Lady' than remembering his lines, or lip-synching on cue. Incandescent with rage, Disney – well known throughout Tinseltown for his paradoxical hatred of animals – had both dogs killed. It was at this moment that Dixie Meech attempted to ingratiate himself with Disney by arranging a birthday puppet show for the great man, starring the dogs' corpses – the ending of which was a deeply macabre *mise-en-scene* of the jigging bodies gobbling up a single strand of spaghetti, and ending with a kiss from beyond the grave. Disney loved it, and immediately began to sketch. The rest is history, as the documentary instead became a light-hearted cartoon love story. The stuffed dogs remain on display in Meech's home – dangling from the partition serving hatch between kitchen and dining room. A proud memento of a lifetime in entertainment.

ANTON LEMEC, BEVERLEY HILLS

Do we really have no bananas?

Ken Chaser, Wellington, New Zealand

Yes.

M. BEARD, DARTMOUTH

No, we do.

B. TAYLOR, BRADFORD

Is it true that a horse was once Pope?

Georgina Difford, London

Much like the myth that Napoleon made his favourite horse, Marengo, a general, this is a myth. There are lots of stories of animals being given positions of authority, though. Of peculiar interest is the previously lawless town of Fort Johnstone, Utah, which elected a duck as its sheriff in 1889, when no man would take the job. The duck, who was called Clarence, instantly became the most famous law enforcer for hundreds of miles. Billy the Kid passed through the town in this time and, as all citizens were requested to, surrendered his firearms to the Sheriff's deputy. Clarence's celebrity grew and he revelled in it – by the spring of 1890 he was only leaving O'Sullivan's Saloon to dip his head in the river and freshen up. He took up with a dancer called Monty Schoolgirl and groups of people visited the town only to see him in action, which boosted the economy.

But such fame has its consequences. A notorious outlaw and jail escapee, Chips Dooley, took the perceived success of the mallard to heart. In his gang's robbery of the bank in Coeur d'Alene, Idaho, in 1886 his brother had tripped over a duck, got caught and been hanged in the town square. Dooley rode into Fort Johnstone, refusing to give up his gun, and bragged loudly in the saloon that he was there to set up a Chinese restaurant. People rushed to Clarence in

114

concern for his life and he was smuggled out of town on the daybreak train the next morning, in a large lady's handbag. It's from this event that we get today's phrase 'handbags at dawn'.

Countless versions of this tale have sprung up over the years. In some Dooley catches the duck, cooks him and dies choking on a bone. In at least one Dooley sets eyes on Clarence for the first time, gives up his wicked ways and they go off to start a farm together. But the truth is more prosaic: Clarence travelled across the country to San Francisco, where he successfully set up office as a lawyer and, in old age, consulted on the many early movie versions of his life. He died there in 1931.

LAWRENCE CHAGRIN, LA TOURNEUSE, LOUISIANA

In response to the above answer, I should say that it's not just animals that are sometimes placed in positions of responsibility. At my local comprehensive in the late eighties, after a fresh batch of debilitating cutbacks, our head of English was unable to replace a leaving teacher, and left us in the charge of an apple from his briefcase. I think he'd been finding his job very stressful.

What we found was that after a few weeks of messing around we got very bored with our own games and pisstaking and eventually fell to reading the books on the shelves. Long arguments came out of what we thought about the texts, and eventually we would take it in turns to describe on the board what we felt each book was trying to say. By the end of the year we knew the set texts, and indeed all of the literary canon that came within the limits of Battersea Park High School's book budget, incredibly well. Most of us still look back on those few months as a bright shaft of light in our educations. Our results were the best the school had seen, and we all thought the apple the best teacher we had ever had. At a reunion a few years ago it didn't surprise me at all to learn that the apple had eventually made it to headmaster.

J. PUGH, ROCHESTER

I won't add much to the two previous enlightening responses except to point out that it hasn't always been members of the animal and vegetable kingdoms that have been elevated to positions of authority. A Scottish distillery was once controversially left, in the will of its previous owner, to a favourite pitching wedge. The case has dragged out for over thirty years in the Scottish courts, and several of the litigants have died of old age. The pitching wedge is polished once a month and remains undefeated, now on its fourteenth set of lawyers.

Another case is that of the Norwegian expedition to the Antarctic in 1952 where the members suffered a mass delusion through the cold and voted to replace as their leader the sense that someone's just left a room when you go in. Shortly afterwards they fell to killing and eating one another. More surprisingly, it was recently revealed in the diaries of her personal doctor that in the last and most infirm years of her reign, Queen Victoria repeatedly abdicated her throne for spells of a few days at a time to 'the wingèd serpent O and his army of suppurating mouth-goblins'.

GREG STRAND, BRIGHTON

What do NASA scientists say instead of 'It's not rocket science, you know'?

Paul Carrel, Berlin

NASA is, contrary to the version put forward in movies such as *Apollo 13*, almost exclusively populated by beautiful women. I was disturbed when I worked there briefly a few years ago to find it an acidly bitchy environment. Peopled with super-achieving bombshells who do their day's work in ten minutes then paint their nails and gossip about celebs rather than appear to try at being brilliant, it was certainly a challenge to fit in. A favourite pastime was finding new stars or constellations and naming them insultingly after former boyfriends (Floppy Phil and Try Again Tony remain, to the chagrin of astronomers around the world, solar systems in the Useless Men Galaxy, to be found on star charts within the Coma Berenices constellation). Hearing that Whitney Houston had checked into rehab, my only ever joke ('Houston, we have a problem') went down leader than a dead balloon.

They did, however, have lots of expressions of contempt. Few of us escaped scorn from the ultra-talented elite, but if someone showed a lack of capability remarks would range from 'It's hardly retrographing a quasic spectrochart, darling' to 'Maybe that explains you wearing that tie with that shirt, sweetie'.

On launch day it was amazing, though, how these über-cynics rose as one woman to admire the spectacle of a three-hundred-foot rocket roaring into the heavens with unimaginable, relentless power. At that moment, I myself discovered stirrings I had never foreseen, and ended up moving to San Francisco to work in a bar. All those people working hour after hour for years on end to prepare this erect engine to impregnate the skies. Think they did it for their CVs? Come on. It's hardly brain surgery.

COREY MAPLEBLOSSOM, SAN FRANCISCO, CA

Why is there only one Monopoly Commission?

Hilary Shylace, Cantank, Missouri

Members of the Monopoly Committee have fallen in the line of duty by the dozen. Since it was founded in 1936 in the depths of the Depression, the Committee has honoured the challenge set out by the game's originator Charles Darrow. Darrow wanted to make a game that would help his effete drinking buddies to plan ever more ambitious debauches around the streets, stations and utilities of their home town. The first version was set in the financial district of Chicago and the concept of developing houses and hotels was anathema to its enjoyment. Darrow was a devoted and highly read Leninist who also happened to be heir to a vast diarrhoea-pill fortune. His dismay after the game appeared in local toy shops and unexpectedly flourished as a paradigm of capitalist endeavour drove him to abandon political thought and live in silence in a monastery.

The game's popularity spread after the newspapers mentioned it was found on Al Capone's table at his 1937 arrest. A true capitalist, Capone sued and won over $100,000 from the Chicago taxpayers: the street soup kitchens shut down later that year, and vagrant deaths reached an all-time high.

It has always remained a favourite of criminals – a set was found in the closet of Carlos the Jackal on his arrest in 1994 in the Sudan after being sedated for an operation on his testicles. For years before he shot John Lennon, Mark David Chapman was also a keen frequenter of the tables in New York's Central Park, where open-air games would continue for months on end.

In accordance with Charles Darrow's original wishes, the Monopoly Committee remains as the body whose job it is to prove in each new city that all the locations on the board can be visited in the course of a single pub crawl. It's a dangerous task, though: at least one member is hospitalised or permanently crippled at each attempt and it has become almost impossible to gain life insurance for members of the Committee. Nevertheless waiting lists are very long and places are extremely hard to get. Another Monopoly Committee sprang up in opposition to us but disbanded during their freshman attempt. I think they then formed a Cluedo Committee – that would be an easier pub crawl, obviously – and that's why there's only one.

PETER PERRYWATER, BEVERLY HILLS, CA

Not so. The Monopoly Commission was, on the contrary, set up by Interpol as a response to the famous 'Boardgame murders' that held America in an airless vice of fear in the long hot summer of 1967. On the third of June that year, a boy out walking his puppy found the body of a man, pierced in a thousand places by what appeared to be long, plastic cocktail sticks, his mouth filled with bloodied marbles. 'KER-PLUNK!' said a crude sign made out in ripped newspaper letters, pinned to the man's chest. As the county police floundered for a lead, more bodies began to turn up: an elderly professor, killed with a candlestick in his local library; a young woman devoured by hungry hippos in the Kansas City wildlife park; and a hideously botched killing that referenced Yahtzee – botched, that is, because nobody has ever worked out how the bloody game is played, which clearly frustrated the murderer as much as the people who bought the game. The murders were never solved, but to this day naughty children throughout middle America are warned that if they don't behave, they'll get Scrabbled. Of course, here in Britain the European branch of the Monopoly Commission has very little to do in real terms. Last week I served an ASBO on some hoodies who were playing 'Buckaroo' by hanging garden furniture on elephants at the local zoo, but I'm glad to say that here in the UK, most people play by the rules.

OFFICER GEOFF CHEUNG, SOMERSET BRANCH OF
THE MONOPOLY COMMISSION

There is only one Monotony Commission. I do not know why, but there is. I have been a member for fourteen years. I like it. The biscuits in the meetings are very nice, butter biscuits, not made with margarine, which I think you can taste even in 'quality' biscuits you see in supermarkets these days, it stays on the tongue like a sticky paste. Margarine, I mean. Rather than monotony. I think monotony is essential to calm living and being a fully rounded person. I hope you publish my letter. Thank you.

JASQUITH P. P. S. LINTEL, NEW MALDEN

[Ed note: Fucking hell, Penny. We don't have to publish everything we get, do we? Why not print the first thing that comes to hand – one of my invoices from Soho Video & Books, for instance, or the contents of the old tissue I found in the pocket of my jacket this morning? Get out of the office, girl, get some fresh air. I'm not a total ogre, you know. I'll survive until you get back. Buy a dress, get a haircut (for God's sake get a haircut!). And while I'm about it, label that disgusting soya stuff you leave in the fridge – I put some in my tea on Tues and would have called an ambulance if I could remember the blasted number. I coughed, snorted it through my nose, broke a blood vessel and had to staunch it with my 'mouse mat' as you call it.]

My best mate reckons that if he eats the right foods, he can do a hollow turd. Is he telling the truth?

James Burke, Cornwall

No.

SAMANTHA JEPPER, DEPT OF BIOLOGY, UNIVERSITY OF KENDAL

No.

PARK WO JONG, DIRECTOR, INSTITUTE OF BOWEL RESEARCH, SEOUL

It has been documented in some research facilities that certain breeds of primate, kept for some time on a specific diet of pulses, can . . . I can't keep this up. No. That's ridiculous.

KEN POWELL, SECRETARY, SPECIAL INVESTIGATIVE COMMITTEE ON VEGETABLE AND HUMAN WASTE RECYCLING, GLOS

My daughter recently showed me that by pressing different keys on my computer I can create 'short cuts' – but for the life of me I cannot replicate her prowess. How can I achieve this?

Col. Henry Bofaloff-Standesque, Sharpington

Like an earlier questioner, I believe you've written into the wrong question/answer column, as this is not the problem page of *PC Today*. You may be interested to know, however, that hitting Ctrl-Alt-Home-T makes the legend HAIRY PONCE jump up on the screen in flashing green letters.

G. TULIP, ANTWERP

There are more short cuts on your PC than you may ever know. This is thanks to a rogue software engineer who worked for Microsoft in the early days and hardwired a variety of eccentricities too deep into the Word program for them ever to be removed. He had a personal grudge against his parents which went back to his baptism, when he had been blessed with the name Felix Happywell – a name which, as a dedicated miserabilist and grump, he despised. He was, however, a programmer extraordinaire and was taken on as one of the first developers of Microsoft's most ubiquitous program, quickly imbuing it, aside from a host of user-friendly and time-saving features, with impossible-to-detect messages of hate and hardware instructions of extraordinary intricacy. He could, for instance, begin running his bath by pressing Shift-/-M-#-B, or, by holding down Ctrl-Shift-F4, cause a network of light bulbs he had placed on the hill behind the house of a hated co-worker to blaze forth the message GOD HATES YOU, PIG.

His subterfuge and decidedly unMicrosoftian behaviour was discovered one day when he fell asleep at his desk and his face slumped onto his keyboard, holding down the keys that eliminated his credit card bill, and wiping the bank accounts of the entire populace of the Bay Area in San Francisco.

His imbedded instructions are still coming to light. To this day, for instance, pressing Alt-Shift-T-Space-Tab makes every key on your computer produce a honking noise. You can still, also, send a huge surge of electricity through your monitor, causing it to hop amusingly off your desk, by holding down Ctrl-Caps lock-Alt-S-P-U-T-U-M.

Happywell disappeared into an ashram for ten years after the controversy over his dismissal, but is rumoured to have surfaced on the Net in recent years under a variety of monickers, and to have accidentally started the Iraq war by pressing Ctrl-Enter-F-Alt-Space-B.

ERNESTO SHAMS, GREENWRICH

Is it a cliché to say that a phrase is 'something of a cliché'?

John Evans, Greater London

Is the Pope Catholic? No man would be prouder of this irony than the man who brought more joyless prose to the world than any other: the late, great mad hatter of modern language teaching, Professor Timothy Taunton. An idiot savant tragically lacking in the 'savant' half of the package, Taunton was not a man to let sleeping dogs lie. From his pied-á-terre in the charming seaside resort of Brighton, the professor made it his raison d'être to take overblown language by the scruff of the neck and produce something far more middle of the road, like a rabbit from a hat. Getting people's backs up was his bread and butter, but harder to swallow was the fact that Taunton's life itself began to take the form of a cliché. After finding a hair in his soup at his favourite restaurant (and instantly informing the waiter), something snapped in Taunton's mind – the straw that broke the camel's back, as it were. Shooting his mouth off at his fellow diners, using language that would make a whore blush, the mad professor ran hell for leather into the street, stripped to his birthday suit and made for the beach like a demented Reginald Perrin. Whether or not he forged into the crashing waves with the intention of doing himself a mischief is not known; what will go down in history is his final words to the onlooking crowd, who looked on aghast as he dived in, came up for air and gave the strangled cry: 'Come on in, the water's lovely!'

WHICH TYLER, KENT

If one synchronised swimmer drowns, do they all have to drown?

Mark Chott, London

Did the questioner not watch the tragic Moscow Olympics of 1980? The much-feared Soviet team came out into the stark strip lighting of the main swimming hall and lined up alongside the pool with almost machine-like precision, resplendent in their bright red costumes and yellow caps. As the first chords of Queen's 'Fat-Bottomed Girls' struck up from the tannoy, the lead Soviet swimmer, Olga Snuffskaya, turned a perfectly pointed ankle towards the international panel of judges . . . and slipped, falling into the water with a strangled cry before drowning horribly. Perfectly drilled by hundreds of hours in the pool together, all eight members of the Soviet team immediately saluted the crowd with their matchless communist ankles, raised their arms to the ceiling, and crashed into the pool with all the grace of a herd of cows. Observing the event, Philip Larkin noted it had 'a kind of murderous bovine poetry to it'. The crowd was silent. Freddie Mercury sang on. No more bubbles rose. And then, convinced that what they had seen was the first truly postmodern display in Olympic history, the judges awarded a perfect set of 6.0 scores, and the crowd went potty. With the bar set at an impossible level, the subsequent teams from South Korea, Fiji, Japan and the Isle of Sheppey had no choice but to follow suit and commit Olympic hara-kiri in a dash for medals. One hundred and seventy-four young women who will be much missed, and a stark reminder of the dangers of dancing underwater.

STEVE NORTH, QUIMSITCH, NORFOLK

W hat is the real origin of the term 'Prince Albert'? I presume it has nothing to do with the royal consort?

Tom Wharton, London

Happily for those of us with a ruder sense of humour, the 'Prince Albert' style of piercing, whereby a ring through the foreskin keeps a man's 'outline' flat against his trouser front, can indeed be traced back to the fashion decisions of Queen Victoria's beloved husband. What is not widely known is that, upon Albert's death, Victoria insisted that a huge, phallic monument to her priapic partner, topped by a shining golden ring, be erected (. . .) in Hyde Park, entirely at the public's expense. The royal command was put to Parliament, but immediately became bogged down in a series of cross-party committees when it became clear that such a magnificent memorial would cost some £20 (£4 million in today's money). Eventually the Queen regally withdrew from the argument, accepted a much plainer plan, said nothing more on the matter and retired to Osborne House to smoke and play rummy. The matter was soon forgotten, and the memorial we know today was created: a steepling tower, with Albert's golden figure seated upon a throne. And that was the end of that. Or was it? For, strolling past the Albert Hall last week with my wife, I looked up at the tremendous bell-shaped dome of the Hall – encircled by a magnificent golden band, a shining ring of metallic fire – and couldn't help but wonder whether the wily old Queen hadn't won the argument after all . . .

REGINALD STOAT, CHELSEA

Is it possible to exist on a diet consisting solely of one type of foodstuff?

Staff Nurse Patricia Womb, Northants.

In a bizarre and famous case in Finland in the 1950s the members of the cult of Jorgen Jespersen, who believed himself to be the reincarnation of Jesus Christ, took to eating one foodstuff each to counteract the 'conspiracy of poison' whereby they claimed governments controlled the minds of their subjects through drugs placed in foods. After the grounds of his sizeable mansion outside Hjetssberg, near the city of Kokkola, were stormed by the national guard on 3 February 1957, extensive notes were found and eventually published in several science journals. They can make for amusing, if not particularly pleasant, reading.

There is a note of levity in the case notes of Arne J. Smit, whose dedicated food was sweetcorn. His (now often-quoted) complaint against the experiment was that his faeces consisted exclusively of the undigested buds of sweetcorn, and that sometimes he could 'look down and not know whether that was what I ate yesterday, or tonight's supper'. His surname subsequently became a term of playground abuse in Finland to describe an imbecile, vagrant or dirty person.

Things were not so light-hearted for his comrade Maria Enwuld, who succeeded in voiding an entire pine cone and subsequently bled to death.

It is interesting to note that Jespersen attributed his ability to see these truths to his superior powers of perception, and therefore deemed it unnecessary that he restrict his own diet or take part in the experiment. He was imprisoned for kidnapping and unlawful possession of restricted poisons and took his life in 1962, aged forty. At this point, with genetically modified crops still years away, in many ways the ideas of Jespersen were ahead of their time. But the religious mania was as old as the hills.

PROF. J. P. MUTTILL, ONKSBIG, FINLAND

I was most interested to read Professor Muttill's learned letter in last month's issue concerning the digestion (or lack thereof) of various foodstuffs. Further to the professor's answer, I can attest that if one eats a diet solely consisting of sweetcorn, as my wife and I have done for the last three years, one's faecal matter does indeed come to be composed entirely of sweetcorn, and nothing but sweetcorn. I am now too weak to walk up the stairs unaided and, as I write, my wife is a funny shade of yellow, but the whole experiment has certainly made for a brighter sight in one's morning toilet than boring old brown.

CHARLES MERRYWEATHER, SUFFOLK

Is Beckham a bender?

Anna Valdinger, Czech Republic

[Ed note: A good number of our older readers wrote in with variants of this question, protesting at the national advertising campaign for the film Bend it Like Beckham *– many had assumed it to be a 'blue' movie. I can assure our readers that there is no cause for alarm; Mr Beckham can do many wonderful things with his golden balls, I am sure, but if we are to believe what we read in the Red Tops, only with members of the opposite sex other than his wife – certainly not with men.]*

Further to earlier answers, readers may recall David Beckham's infamous text exchange with Rebecca Loos, in which the word 'blank' was helpfully inserted by the *Screws of the World*. What many readers may not have noticed was the tabloid's subsequent retraction and apology some months later, when they were forced to provide a full transcript of the end of the text exchange. Suddenly, the whole thing read slightly differently:

> 'Remember what I done to you when I put my blank up your blank, and moved it about a bit? It was amazing, blank was streaming out of it, but I just kept blanking, and then putting the blank all over your blank until it clogged it completely. Then I blanked the end of it – really, really gently – and suddenly there was a massive blank, and we were both covered in blank. I can tell you, the next time you have that problem in your bathroom, I'm calling a plumber.

PAUL DREW, STOKE NEWINGTON

How much can I get away with and still go to Heaven?

Quentin Roundtree, County Roscommon, Eire

It appears we Catholics have got a nice little number going here as the theoretical answer is: any amount. But practically speaking, any sinner genuinely repenting of his or her sin has to come to a humane appreciation of what they've done. By that rule, Hitler, for example, could gain God's favour by truly and humbly appreciating the

131

magnitude of the evil he had brought about and begging forgiveness, but it would probably take about thirty million years to get enough information into his mind for him to understand what he did. By the same rule, if newspapers are to be believed, most priests would need to live to a couple of thousand years old at least.

MATTHEW M. L. JOHN, ROME

The self-styled mystic and mindreader 'Fabuloso Ali BaBa' – a hit with London theatre audiences throughout the late 1890s – is known to have used this catchphrase question to promote what were, by Victorian standards, fantastically lewd vaudeville shows. BaBa is said to have begun each performance by appearing, in a puff of smoke, from the top of an enormous papier mâché penis, with a cry of 'By Pharaoh's beard, how much can I get away with and still go to Heaven?' Posters in florid typography trumpeted the question from every street corner, and the catchphrase soon spread to become something of a phenomenon among the upper classes (the Belgian Ambassador Extraordinary and Plenipotentiary to London is said to have made a grab at Queen Victoria's majesterial bosom while drunk at a party; despite having winked at the crowd hopefully while being lead away, shouting, 'How much can I get away with and still go to Heaven?', the poor ambassador was summarily thrown into the River Thames, and the incident led to a minor war with the low countries).

In the final analysis, however, modern readers will find BaBa's stunts remarkably tame. His 'unforgivable' sins included shouting 'D__ Prince Albert!' (he couldn't bring himself to get past the 'D'); a full back tattoo of a beaver with the words 'HellO there' tattooed on his backside, the 'O' of 'hello' being formed by the shrivelled red starburst of his sphincter; and a song-and-dance number involving twelve Alexandrian dancing girls and a 'Terrible African snake' – which was actually a poorly disguised and rather mangy sausage dog called Toby, in a mask. BaBa's act soon went out of fashion, though his tattoo design, of course, went on to be made famous in the twentieth century by the tattooist Sailor Jerry, who swapped the beaver for a chimpanzee saying, 'ALOHA'.

Why did Hitler have such a silly moustache?

Felicity Pilkington, London

Not many people realise that Hitler had only peripheral vision for most of his adult life. Forever bumping into lampposts in his native Austria, slung out of art school for painting strange pictures with a stripe of blank canvas down the middle, it is amazing that none of his advisers picked up on the problem when the Nazis assumed real power in the 1930s. Not even his closest adjutants could have known that every morning, while shaving, Hitler (understandably) took a blade only to that part of his face that he could safely see – that is, everything outside of the central inch of his reflection. But this is small beer. Who knows how the war might have turned out, had Hitler been able to see what was directly in front of his face? Poring over maps of Europe with Goering in 1938, it is well documented that Hitler was seemingly unable to concentrate on Germany – forever pointing to the left and right of it and shouting, 'This is my country!' Generals and adjutants were said to have immediately scurried off and issued orders to invade Poland and France. The rest is history.

NORMAN SIDEWELL, DIPCOTT

Hitler's moustache has become the source of much debate between those who think they remember him having one, to mischievous 'moustache deniers' who contend that Hitler was utterly incapable of growing facial hair. When confronted by the evidence of millions of feet of film showing the famous clipped inch of authoritarian bristle, historian Darren Irving (no relation to the Holocaust denier David) has contested – with no little support from French scholars – that each frame of celluloid, *every single photograph taken of the Führer* from 1922 to 1945, had a moustache added by hand, to make him appear more manly. If Irving is to be believed, Albert Speer was diverting up to 300,000 Bulgarian workers away from the magnesium mines in late 1944, solely to concentrate on scribbling moustaches on to photographs.

Whatever the true answer, it is interesting to note that moustache-denial (*taschengenichtsagen*) is actively encouraged by the governments of both Germany and Austria, in stark contrast to their stark legal stand on Holocaust denial.

SHONA CAREW, INSTITUTE OF FACIAL STUDIES, BELFAST

D oes the Queen really go to the toilet like the rest of us?

Billy Braithwaite, aged ten, London

Well, Billy, I can tell you for certain that Queen Victoria didn't. Although she never suffered from porphyria like poor George III, in the years after the death of her beloved Albert she suffered panic attacks, and would become temporarily insane. The onset was marked by rapid shallow breathing and could be detected by her helpers, who would rush her out of public if they saw the signs. There was nothing to be done when an attack came on during a performance of *Twelfth Night* in 1879, however, and in her confusion she launched onto the stage, flinging handfuls of her own excrement, shouting what the cast later called 'vile untruths', threw off her clothes and hurled herself at the actor playing Viola who, in her disguise as a man, she took to be Albert. The packed audience then discovered the royal couple's most intimate secret as she unburdened her bladder over the actress's fake beard and horror-stricken mouth.

Other rulers have had toilet trouble over the years – the most unlucky being Roman Emperor Constantine V, who fouled himself during his christening and was dubbed Copronymous. Especially unlucky to go down in history as what translates as 'Name of Shit', when by all accounts he was a good leader, perfectly nice bloke and enthusiast of the pipe organ, albeit prone to bouts of depression. But who wouldn't be?

BOBBY ROCKSEDGE, LASTING, SHROPS

[Ed note: Penny, I'm sure this isn't true. Look it up, would you? Our readers seem to have something against our greatest Queen, and I don't like it (I don't count Elizabeth I – I can't respect a virgin). By the way, my wife gave me that film you wanted to borrow. It's in the fridge. She said DVDs should be kept refrigerated to be in best condition – I don't know if she was serious, but better to be on the safe side.]

What have the Romans ever done for us?

Matthew Maher, London

Made famous by the Monty Python film *The Life of Brian*, this question affords we classical historians endless amusement, speculating on just how different life would be in modern Europe, had Julius Caesar never set foot in Dover. Who can imagine an England without ceramic cups and saucers, olive oil, antimacassars, Connect Four, dildos, frozen peas and hoodies?

GERALD STATSIN, DEPARTMENT OF DILDO RESEARCH,
AMSTERDAM

More importantly, they have given us the delicious Mr Adam Hart-Davis, and his informative, laugh-out-loud funny variety shows about what the Romans did for us. Mr Hart-Davis is a natural comedian, a charming raconteur and – as last year's tax return 'egg-timer' advertisements showed – absolutely tiny. Bravo, Mr Hart-Davis, for showing us that size does not matter!

RACHEL MANFREDTENDENSON, TWICKENHAM

What is the origin of the word 'mugshot'?

Andy Spue, Middlesbrough

Interestingly, this term actually predates the discovery of photography, referring instead to the method used by eighteenth-century policemen to keep track of known highwaymen on the roads of rural England. Tobias Longfellow, better known as 'Dandy Dick', was the most famous robber of the era – a ruthless man, known for firing first and asking questions later. Eventually, the local sheriff mounted a concerted effort to bring Longfellow to justice – and upon capturing him, ordered a lightning-fast tapestry of his likeness to be made by the Norwich Embroidery Circle. After some four weeks of stitching the decorative border, Longfellow saw his opportunity, evaded the clutching old seamstresses, and made good his escape.

Enraged, the sheriff redoubled his efforts to catch 'Dandy Dick', and after a tremendous chase across half the counties in England, caught him and ordered a local potter to throw an instant likeness of the robber. This time it worked – within minutes, twenty copies of Longfellow's cruel, scarred sneer were cast and stuck to the front of drinking tankards, to be hung from the ceilings of public houses up and down the highways of England. Old Tobias's likeness therefore found both fame and infamy and we still see 'Toby jugs' – or 'mugshots' – today, hanging from the walls of pubs.

MARIE SHOALS, SHROPS

[Ed note: Penny. Oh dear. Afraid I came back to the office in rather a state last night after a barnstorming lunch with old Harry W. Not feeling jolly at all – hope I didn't do anything I shouldn't have. Be an angel and bring the rug to put round my shoulders and some of that fruit stuff you drink. There's a good girl.]

What is the perfect crime?

Jules Cowper, Bloomsbury, London

I am in the process of committing it, and I choose to do so in public, here on the letters page of this wretched rag. The crime will be perfect since everyone shall know of it, but none shall prevent it. And in the process, I shall utterly discredit that meddling hag Miss Marbles for the last time! Look about you, old woman. The cat is on the prowl.

DR MORIARTÉ, POSTMARKED 'SECRET LAIR', UPPER MUFFINGTON,

SOMERSET

We meet again, Moriarté. Readers will no doubt wish to know that, since the letter of my old nemesis was posted, a murder has been committed in the library of the vicarage in Lower Muffington. My dear, poor Moriarté, how simplistic of you! How could you have thought that I might miss the fact that the reverend's brightly coloured macaw had been trained to speak but one word of Italian – *minchia* – a command that set the vicar's own Yorkshire terriers upon him without mercy. I have passed on these details to the Lower Muffington constabulary, and await your next move. As I said to Lady Swithingham while idly playing with her succulent chopped liver, this wily old dog is in need of no new tricks, and awaits your move with interest.

MISS MARBLES, LOWER MUFFINGTON, SOMERSET

Poor, barren, tweed-encased old harridan. My fame increases with every letter, and you are no closer to discovering my real crime. The snake stirs in his lair. You will know the marks of his bite.

DR MORIARTÉ, POSTMARKED 'SECRET LAIR', WITH A HANDWRITTEN

NOTE ON THE ENVELOPE: POSTMASTER: PLEASE REFRAIN FROM

ADDING 'UPPER MUFFINGTON' TO THE POSTAL STAMP, IF YOU WANT A

Dear, silly Frenchman! The second murder, in old Mr
Tumble's shop on Little Twittering high street, was child's
play itself to solve. As I remarked to my friend the colonel
before I placed my lips around his trumpet, the glass from
the broken window lay outside the shop, instantly ruling
out a burglar; and naturally, it was perfectly impossible for a
trained nose not to smell the faint whiff of almonds in
Tumble's tea – cyanide! Or poisoned almonds. Either way,
the mosquito net is tightening, Moriarté. I shall patiently
sit and play with Mrs Tennyson's beaver, awaiting next
month's issue of the *Old Git* with interest.

MISS MARBLES, LOWER MUFFINGTON, SOMERSET

You do go on, you old bitch. But you raise an interesting
question. Whose net is tightening? Who is the fisherman,
and who the fish? The perfect crime draws close.

DR MORIARTÉ, POSTMARKED 'SECRET LAIR', AGAIN WITH A
HANDWRITTEN NOTE: TO THE EDITOR: PLEASE TELL YOUR IDIOT
SECRETARY TO STOP TYPING UP EVERY WRITTEN WORD THAT IS PUT
IN FRONT OF HER – INCLUDING THE ADDRESS OF MY SECRET LAIR!
AT THIS RATE, I MIGHT AS WELL WRITE 'MORIARTÉ, 8, PEBBLE LANE,
UPPER MUFFINGTON' AND SIMPLY INVITE THE POLICE TO COME AND
TAKE ME! YOURS, STEFAN MORIARTÉ. AND CAN NONE OF YOU
LACKWITS SPELL 'CLARIFICATIONS'?

*[Ed note: Penny, do please do as the man says. The exchange
has been terribly exciting so far. By the way, this almond
croissant is excellent. Did you get it from the little place on*

the corner run by the funny little Italian and his brother? I
don't see how they can *be brothers, though, with the younger*
one being taller and blonde and so much younger. Different
fathers perhaps. Yummy yummy yummy, anyway.]

The old eagle does so enjoy toying with her dear, arrogant
vole. Even you could not eat an entire undefrosted lamb
chop in order to dispose of the bludgeoning murder
weapon that did for the milliner's wife in Piddleswater last
Wednesday.

I am but a poor old woman, with too much time to read,
and I have read Borges. I know, then, that the three
murders so far chart three points on the map; and that you
intend for me to meet you at the fourth point of a perfect
diamond, at my home in Lower Muffington, in order to kill
me. I shall be waiting for you with a heavily armed
squadron of policemen, Moriarté – and I shall have won the
game. As I said to the Baroness as I parted her beef curtains
(unusual, but delicious), I shall hand this letter over to the
postman with a skip and a hop; days later, it will be
published, and I may retire. How do you like those rich,
rosy apples?

ENID MARBLES, LOWER MUFFINGTON

I knew, of course, that the dear readers of these letters
would know that I knew that she had read Borges. I also
knew that the old crone would not be able to resist
writing one final letter to the magazine, the letter that
sealed the fate of her boastful reputation. For the last
two months, I have dressed as the local postman, having
killed the credulous fool weeks ago for making the

address of my secret lair known. Nobody ever notices the postman – especially the poor, defunct, very dead Miss Marbles . . .

DR MORIARTÉ, HM PRISON, PENTONVILLE. THE ENVELOPE IS MARKED: **DO NOT DARE** WRITE THE POSTMARK THIS TIME. FOR THE CRIME TO BE PERFECT, ALL MUST ASSUME THAT I WAS NOT PICKED UP BY THE POLICE, THANKS TO WRETCHED PENNY'S INABILITY TO SELF-EDIT WHAT SHE IS GIVEN TO TYPE. I SHALL HAVE MY REVENGE!

Unfortunately I note the laboured prose style of my colleague D. Dumble in the foregoing missives. His quest to find a gullible enough publisher for his embarrassing 'Murders in Philpott' series of detective novels remains forlorn. Barely a week goes by without him flinging another rejection letter to one side with that strangled choking noise he knows I hate. Reclaiming the last from the wastepaper basket, I found the letter to be not a rejection slip but an editor's resignation, unable to stand another word. He has also seen fit to ignore my point that, in *Murder Takes a Bath*, from which tiresome story the above is cribbed, the locations of the murders do not join up on the map to show a diamond shape, but something which if it looks like anything is closer to a toilet brush. Aside from the characterisation, which is neither convincing nor likable, the murder and its solution are shamelessly lifted from Conan Doyle's 'The Case of Oranges'.

I remain ever your humble,

PROF. H. H. UNSELF, BROCKHAMPTON

Well now, I appear to have been rumbled; and only time shall tell if my game attempts at fiendishly constructed crime fiction see the light of day that they deserve. But in the spirit of openness afforded by my dear, drear office mate, perhaps I can share with readers the source of much hilarity in the pubs of Brockhampton this last month: H. H. Unself's as-yet-unpublished 'erotic saga' *The Crack of Dawn*, which I chanced upon quite innocently while systematically burning old H. H's papers.

This racy debut by one 'Candice de la Mare' is a stunningly ill-conceived bodice-ripper set in the famous Devil's Island penal colony of French Guiana in the 1930s. In the book's opening its heroine, the beautiful Dawn Décolletage, wife to the prison's hard-faced governor, returns flushed from a passionate encounter at the top of a palm tree in her private garden:

> *How Dawn wished that she could be there with him still: a tough, brutish man and a murderer to boot, but a man all the same, with a firm, muscled body toned by twenty years of hard manual labour. All through dinner, a lavish spread laid on for the warders and their wives, Dawn could not help but sigh and think of Pierre lifting her in his brawny arms; of his rough handling as he carried her to the top of the tree, grasping at her coconuts with the hunger of a man who has known much suffering in this world . . .*

I shall leave it to the readers of the *Old Git* to judge the merits of Unself's scribblings; while I withdraw gracefully to continue my own magnum opus, happy in the knowledge that I remain, sir,

PROF. DUMBLE, BROCKHAMPTON

I, in turn, must acknowledge myself exposed in my literary pretensions. But hopefully mine will not be deemed so empty a project as Dumble's woebegotten bothering of Agatha Christie's ghost. Dawn Décolletage is to appear in a number of adventures according to my current plans, becoming reborn with each story in a new time and place.

I have her in the court of Louis XVI as Marie Antoinette's maid, undergoing a sentimental education with the King and finally opening her legs, faced with a ravenous peasant horde, to cry, 'Let them eat ME!' (I abandoned an anachronistic affair with Chopin to lever in the under-the-piano phrase 'aprés moi le prelude'.)

I have her experiencing a renaisssance of her own posing as a model for Florentine artists in the sixteenth century and explaining both Michelangelo's ability to lie flat for two years while he painted the ceiling of the Sistine Chapel as well as the Mona Lisa's reluctant beginning of a smile . . .

I have her reborn on Sapphos, discovering the love that blooms between a goatherd milkmaid and a starving peasantgirl in a volume I intend to name *Rosie Fingered Dawn* . . .

I shall bring the sequence to a climax where Dawn appears at a Midlands university and becomes friends with two ageing professors, marrying first one then the other, before finding that in the squirm and sordor of academic life these souls – unprepossessing in looks, perhaps even 'unattractive' by the corrupt standards of our media age – deserve and desire one another. That despite the Trafalgan crossfire that splits the air in their tiny office they cannot live without each other. At the desk, in the kitchen or beneath the sheets of the bed from whose centre they have only recently had the courage to remove the dead weight of Dawn's wooden leg, they unite in late-flowering adoration. This volume, entitled *A Dawn at Dusk*, is the most sober, and hopefully the most moving of the series.

Humbly I submit its outline as a reflection on my previous missives, which I hope may seem altered by the light of its new dawn.

I remain, ever, your servant

H. H. UNSELF

If a monkey farts, does it smell like bananas?

Father Herbie Sparkling, Dallas, TX

Put it this way: if you eat nothing but oranges for six hours, and then go for a piss, does it smell like you're an idiot?

IRIS PEACE, ARNOS GROVE

What if there were no hypothetical questions?

Adam Armsrib, Seven Sisters

[Ed note: Penny, no reply to this one? Here's a hypothetical question for you. What would happen if you read these stupid questions before we print them? If there were no hypothetical questions, we'd have to pay someone to fill this space with writing that is actually about something. *The thought makes me cold all over – turn up the heating and make up the bed in the photocopier room, would you, I got onto the Falklands War over dinner last night and the old girl's chucked me out again.]*

Does anyone actually read the *Screws of the World*, or do they just look at the pictures?

E. Cramp, County Durham

Honestly? We here at the *Screws* hope not! To be frank, not much happens of any interest in Britain any more. The odd cat up a tree here, a cake-judging competition there, an ASBO if you're lucky. Nobody has sex any more, nobody takes drugs . . . We can't exactly make stories up, but we do our best to distract the reader with bold words that CRY out EXCITING things and CATCH the eye. Look at last

146

week's issue, for instance. Headline: 'SMACK MY BITCH UP', accompanied by a picture of a young model in lingerie. It was actually a piece on the hard-fought toy-dog section of Crufts, which was won by a fiesty Chihuahua called Shirley who wouldn't come to heel:

> An onlooker was heard to say: 'Shirley was loving it. Honestly, she's a dog but she was going at it like knives in the walkround section.' A source confirmed that the crowd gasped as Shirley's owner:
>
> **KILLED** time between rounds by lighting up in a non-smoking area
>
> **BONKED** the cheeky dog over the head with an inflatable hammer whenever she refused to sit and
>
> **INVEIGLED** her way into the final group through flattery and keeping Shirley's glossy coat in top condition.

The last time we actually had a sex scandal was in 1974, but restrictions on reporting were so strict back then that we had to make it look like a dog show to get it through the censors. Who'd be a journalist!

MIKE SNARE, EDITORIAL DESK, *SCREWS OF THE WORLD*

[Ed note: This letter originally appeared in the Guardian, *who covered the story of the* Screws of the World's *constant recourse to filth with a pithy 'think' piece, and no fewer than five pages of nude photographs to illustrate the point.]*

Do worms turn?

Lucy Scrimshaw, London

They do, of course, otherwise the fact that they are the most bendy creatures in nature would be a waste. Worms are much misunderstood, and more threatening than we might suppose. Around half of the piles of earth we find in our gardens are not, as we suppose, due to moles, but worms in the sexual frenzy brought on by a heavy rain, searching for other worm contact, finding their own tails and invading.

Worms contain trace amounts of ammonium nitrate, hydrogen and oxygen (which can be used to make home-grown explosives). By connecting their mouths with their anuses an electrical circuit closes, creating a small underground explosion that can blow puffs of earth up to ten feet from the ground.

Guy Fawkes, a keen naturist from childhood, observed this. He planned to get all the supplies of worms in England beneath the Houses of Parliament on 5 November 1606. He was only foiled by John Why, a stubborn-minded fisherman from Maldon in Essex who reported his lack of bait to the local beadle and constable, who was also his son. Robin Why followed the trail all the way to Westminster and overcame the squeamish concerns of local law-enforcement to raid the basement of the House just in time.

Only the more picturesque (and, to the peasantry at the time, comprehensible) version was made public. Of course Fawkes was not the ringleader but was the patsy of a powerful group of landowner fly-fishing dissidents.

SPIRO AGNEW, SING SING

Theoretically, time-warping wormholes, which could explain various historical mysteries such as the Marie Celeste and the Bermuda Triangle, can turn in on themselves. There are those of us that think this happened in the town of Moncada in Brazil, which was visited by half-American journalist Hank Abrazzo in 1936. He found it totally undeveloped, a time capsule to the famine-ridden era of the conquistadores. He sent scathing and fascinating reports of conditions he found up the river which were published in the Brazilian *Day* magazine at the time, and created a quickly forgotten storm of social concern. Few people remembered them within a year.

Then a man appeared naked in a street in New Mexico in 1948, claiming to be Abrazzo, who had been missing for over ten years. I had met Abrazzo and had a drink with him when we covered the Argentine Copper War in the late twenties, and remembered him a few years older than me. This man had the same face but was in his early twenties, and briefly became a news story himself only, in turn, to become forgotten. I interviewed him at this time and remained unconvinced, thinking perhaps he was Abrazzo's estranged and disturbed young son. He betrayed a desire to return to Moncada.

A few years later I read how Moncada had become one of the new cities in Brazil, how it syphoned off talented young entrepreneurs and 'new money' from the less remote cities owing to its amazing technological advancement. I was better off by then and travelled there only to find the prematurely grey shell of Abrazzo walking with a stick across a grand stone bridge named after himself. He saw my face and laughed at its sudden youthfulness to him. Terrified, I ran from him before he could speak and left the city, the province and finally the country.

Within a few years Moncada had disappeared again. Then more recently I read about wormholes appearing between places and times and wondered if I understood what had happened. I was an established man by then, quite old, and worried I might die without discovering my answer, so undertook the risky journey to find the forgotten town. It took many weeks but eventually I found a mud-spattered ruin on the banks of the Amazon and a small boy called Hank, pulling on my sleeves and asking me for money.

TRUMAN F. PROLAND, SILBER COUNTY, ONTARIO

Why is it 'clarfications' in the title of your monthly letters page, and not 'clarifications'?

Kate Harvey and Tom Penn, unmarked envelope

[Ed note: PENNY! What does it take? Are you determined to bring on another episode of Indonesian flu? Fetch a DICTIONARY, girl, look up CLARIFICATIONS and CORRECT THE MASTHEAD! And kindly do not rearrange my office when I am out of it – I want that Bombay gin back in my out-tray in time for my eleven o'clock pick-me-up or I won't be responsible for my actions (it makes for an invaluable paperweight). That is all. And

DO NOT print this note in the bloody blaspheming bastard column!]

What's so bad about living in a 'nanny state'?

Natasha Rint, London

Hear hear – it doesn't sound like such a bad thing to me, having seen the lovely Estonian one my bridge partner Richard has at the moment. Vote Labour!

JEREMY CLEAVE, TOOTING

I don't often write letters to letters pages, but this jaunty, liberal question and Jeremy Cleave's glib answer had me fair boiling with rage. I'll tell you what's wrong with the nanny state: no part of an Englishman's life remains untouched by the meddling Gordon Brown and his tiny son, David Milliband. From health and safety rules that used up most of my capital last year, to almost weekly visits from various government inspectors, I hardly have any time left to run my farm and care for my animals. It's clear that Mr Brown has never had to herd cats, which is difficult at the best of times. Why don't they spend their time policing the real problems that we're facing today in Britain – namely, the influx of deregulated pornography from the Continent? You can get hold of anything nowadays; one click, and I managed to buy things you wouldn't believe from Holland. Honestly, my garage is now full of the stuff, and it disgusts me. All day I sit and watch it – *The Merry Dwarves of Windsor, The Lion, the Witch and the Whore's Robe, Schindler's Fist* – and does New Labour care?

JEREMY SNIPES, KETTERING

S ome neighbours of mine have recently reported broken eggs on their lawns. Does this mean that the cuckoo is in season?

Sir Geoffrey Beezewater, Lambeth (South Bank), London

[Ed note: Penny – just occurred to me might this be old Geoffy 'Boozewater' Beezewater who taught me at Cambridge? Must be quite an age by now. Look down our newest copy of Who's Who (1978, I think) and have a squint, petal.]

I can happily report that, the naivety of the starling aside, recent flights have gone without a hitch and reports of the cuckoo are typical of fright-tactics used by the owl and the robin.

A. BLUEBIRD, BY HAND

For once, following a succession of safe landings, the bluebird and I agree. The cuckoo is nowhere to be seen and the garden is as harmonious and communicative as ever. I look forward to the starling's trip to Bahrain next week to visit the nest of an exiled chaffinch, Sir Geoffrey will be pleased to discover.

T. STARLING, BY HAND

On the eve of my Middle East flight, of course I would normally be singing happily if the starling hadn't given me the wrong passport, a ridiculous name (Joshua Krapoff?) and plumage fit for a diminutive female shotputter. My masters choose to test me once more by matching me with a feathered prat.

A. BLUEBIRD, BY HAND

The bluebird and the starling are ideal companions, as previous flights have shown. Perhaps they do not understand one another's song. The chaffinch's nest is of the utmost importance; do not let bickering affect the results.

SIR GEOFFREY BEEZEWATER

[Ed note: Doesn't sound like him to be honest, Penny. He was razor-sharp but this bloke seems a bit doddery at best with all this rubbish about birds. Still, do look him up to make sure.]

I can report that the bluebird's wings have been clipped. He suffered an accident on landing and sadly fell from his branch. His last wish was that 'the starling be dispatched, spatchcocked and left for a vulture's snack'. I regret that the contents of the chaffinch's nest will not be here should further bluebirds seek it out. Until next time, I am taking wing.

I. CUCKOO, BAHRAIN

The minister understands the implications of the cuckoo's revenge, starling. Desert the tree at once and return to the birdcage. This causes us great sorrow.

SIR GEOFFREY BEEZEWATER

[Ed note: Forget it, Penny. Clearly not him. This guy's obviously bonkers.]

Why isn't there mouse-flavoured cat food?

Cat Row, Amazon Basin, Brazil

On the contrary, indeed there *is* mouse-flavoured cat food – mountains of the bloody stuff, thanks to the French government's long-held policy of subsidising mouse-ranching operations in the Loire. I myself worked on a mouse ranch during my university gap year in the late eighties, and it's a tough job, I can tell you. Up at 4 a.m., we used small treats such as cheese and raisins to tempt the mice out of their sleeping holes; we milked them before the sun came up; and then led them out into the grain field so they could spend the day exercising and fattening themselves up for the kill.

I hope I can reassure everyone that the mice are dispatched very humanely in such farms – though the cattle prods that we use to stun them admittedly did sometimes cause the mice to burst into flames like Bonfire Night sparklers! Absolutely nothing is wasted, though: the mice are bled into espresso cups, the blood being used to make tiny black puddings; the balls go to make 'budget caviar' for a top supermarket chain; and the rest gets minced up and sold to Whiskery Treats Pet Food Inc. Whiskery don't trade in the UK, but readers should know that getting hold of Continental mouse-flavoured cat food is now as easy as a click on a website!

SHARON WEBBED, LINCOLNSHIRE

I would like to complain in the strongest possible terms about Sharon Webbed's letter, which appeared in last month's issue. For those readers not intimately au fait with issues of animal rights: Sharon *Wedebb* – nice try with the anagram, Sharon – is the CEO and co-founder of Whiskery Treats Pet Food Inc, which has long tried to break into the lucrative UK pet-food market. Knowing that the French government would subsidise a turd if it asked them to, Wedebb moved all operations to France, biding her time until UK cat owners caught up with the Continental market. We at the Mouse Alliance are committed to stopping Wedebb and her inhumane practices, which include *milking the mice by hand*; lasooing any mice attempting to escape the grain field; and a barbaric annual 'rodeo', whereby tiny shrews are dressed as Frenchmen, tied to the mouse's saddle, and raced. This cannot continue, and any readers horrified by the illicit trade in mouse flesh can help our cause by signing our online petition at www.whatpricenicemice.com.

MICHAEL STOAT, BEDS

This doesn't have anything to do with mice-flavoured cat food, but in response to Mike Stoat's answer, there is actually a historical instance of a turd being subsidised by the US government. Jelly Roll Morton, 1920s band leader and the man who claimed to have invented jazz, suffered a severe bout of food poisoning in June 1933 in the middle of his most successful season playing with his Kansas City Stompers around the jazz clubs of the East Coast. While staying in the famous Belmont Parks Hotel in Atlantic City he was served a bad plate of shrimp and in the midst of an hallucinatory bout of vomiting and diarrhoea came up with his most enduring creation, a character called Mr Brown, when, staring into the toilet bowl, its contents began to offer him counsel. Mr Brown became the narrator of a string of hits down in the deep south. Collected on one record, Morton's now incredibly rare *Brown Blues* auctions at anything up to $100,000 and he licensed the character to appear in a sequence of cartoons to play at fleapit cinemas as informational films for the black community. These charming shorts include titles such as *That Communis, He Gon Steal Yo Wife, Don' Trust that Republican Man (He Not Yo Fren)* and *No Jailhouse Cookin for Mr Brown (Cos I Don't Got the Reefer Madness)*. People may still remember his song made popular by the Mazda advert from 1993 featuring Emmanuelle Béart which showed her in a desert whispering the lines from his 1934 song 'Dixie Street Shuffle Stomp Blues':

Baby don't want to see me tonight
Baby don't want me to stay
But everything is gonna be alright
Everything gonna be okay

When Morton died of blood poisoning in Mexico in 1941 his friend Sidney Bechet had a grave dug next to him for Mr Brown, inscribing the stone with the legend he thought appropriate for Morton, who had married nine times and lost a leg to alcoholism:

Ashes to ashes
And dust to dust
If the ladies don't get yer
The whisky must

HARLAN BALZALE, JOBY, MISSISSIPPI

157

My housemate claims to be indifferent to Marmite. Is he weird?

Henry Vincent, Twickenham

He's not weird, Henry, but he might be quite seriously ill. In fact he has dangerously low yeast levels and should seek medical attention at once. Our reaction to Marmite depends on the pituitary gland's ability to produce yeast-metabolising enzymes which, if deficient in any way, can adversely affect our ability to taste. There are handy household ways to test this out. He is likely to find Guinness undrinkable, for instance, but will show no aversion to foodstuffs that naturally inspire disgust in healthy people, such as pickle-lily or Findus Crispy Pancakes.

If it has gone on unchecked for some time the disease may have spread to the taste-receptors in the brain, in which case he will show no repugnance to television programmes featuring June Sarpong or Michael Barrymore. He might listen to Chris Moyles's radio show for enjoyment rather than for a useful jolt of anger-fuelled adrenalin like the rest of us, or read a Jeanette Winterson novel without rolling his eyes, making retching sounds and chewing the cover with impotent rage.

In its most advanced form the disease is incurable, and the victim helpless. The saddest thing is that it is not life-threatening and a sufferer can carry on an apparently normal existence for decades – normal that is except for a willingness to watch Adam Sandler movies, to read celebrity gossip magazines without an air of ironic detachment, or to use as their single criterion for buying music the fact that it has reached number one in the charts. It is a very common condition.

DR MARCUS LAPIS-LAZULI, ARNHELM

Do stupid people get the full effect of alphabet soup?

Tim Langston, Essex

I wouldn't like to guess, but there is a strong literary tradition in the use of this apparently childish food. Evelyn Waugh used to be so disgusted at receiving a plate of the stuff for breakfast, after enjoying a drinkathon with Graham Greene, that he would rearrange the letters into the rudest phrase possible. As he says in a letter to Sonia Orwell, one morning in January 1956, the fog of his hangover lifted for a moment when he found he had the letters for RATHER EAT SOME BRIGHTON ROCK, BUMFACE (though the comma is clearly an invention, unless it was a broken off piece of another letter).

Heinz's etymological snack disappeared from the literary world for some decades after, until Kingsley Amis rashly declared that if his son ever got on the Booker Shortlist he'd take a bath in the stuff. When Martin earned that accolade for *Time's Arrow* in 1991, however, he was forced to carry this out. He discovered too late that his son and Christopher Hitchens had set up a press conference under the pretence that Kingsley was raising money for the Philip Larkin Trust to retile the frontage of Hull University. On seeing the cameras enter the bathroom, the old devil dunked the bottle of Martini which had been at his lips into the cold gruel and exploded into a choleric rage. In the third and most violent paragraph of this tirade (journalists standing, microphones impassively held forward all the while) he stood up, allowing them a fuller view of his body of work than even the most dedicated scholar of postwar British fiction has yet amassed. The incident led to embarrassment on the following day's news and a virulent bout of pneumonia that lasted three weeks.

RICHARD HUNT, CAMBRIDGE

Further to Richard Hunt's letter, readers might like to know that alphabet soup was developed as a direct result of the first blossomings of the Cold War in the late 1940s. Furiously competing with the Americans in all branches of research, the Soviets hit on an ingenious educational filip – alphabetti spaghetti – that sent Communist literacy levels through the roof between the years 1949 and 1952. Half-starved Russian children tucked hungrily into the tasty Cyrillic snack, encouraged to spell out rousing slogans such as 'Eat, be strong, for Mother Russia', and were soon outstripping their American counterparts on all literacy indicator tests.

This triumph of pasta engineering should have been lauded throughout the world. Instead it was greeted with cynicism and scorn from the West, one American commentator drily remarking that 'all this shows is that their Italian chefs are better than our Italian chefs'.

DR CATHERINE ESPINER, WINCHESTER

How long is a yonk?

Sally Dolton, Kingston, Jamaica

Unusually for such a Home Counties English word, 'yonk' actually comes from Yiddish. It entered the language through London's East End's pawn shops, to which middle-class people of reduced circumstances would be driven in the early twentieth century. Thus a wife might ask a guilty husband if he had seen a favoured pair of earrings and he might reply, 'I don't know. I haven't seen them in . . . yonks.'

The original Yiddish expression refers to the hollow gulping sound that a schmuck, schlub or schlemiel would give when asked a question to which he did not know the answer. The swallowing sound would be followed by a family member (or onlooker) announcing, 'Yonk!' and all but the silent party would burst into laughter (cf. pp. 23, 49, 189 of *The Adventures of Augie March* by Saul Bellow). In America the word came to punctuate an awkward silence (such as that following an accidental solecism) or a moment of sly one-upmanship. As such it has been used by both Bart and Homer in *The Simpsons*, who, when stealing something in plain view of its owner, emphasise their cheek by saying, 'Yoink!'

A less charming instance is the region of Yonkers in New York. It took its name from a school for children with what we would now call learning disabilities which was established thanks to a bursary from John Paul Getty in 1916. Jewish (and gentile) children from miles around entertained themselves by scaling the walls and crying, 'Yonkers! Yonkers!' into the grounds. The practice ended (although the name stuck) the following year when a wall collapsed, crushing the legs of twenty-nine children. Reluctantly Getty shelled out again for a leg hospital in a vacant lot between the East Village and Chinatown in Manhattan. The medical attention the kids received was less than perfect, however, because so many medical professionals were tending victims of the Somme and Ypres, and this resulted in their appearing bow-legged, another cruel name-call ('Bowers! Bowers!') and the christening of another New York district – the Bowery.

DAVID SOUTH, MERSEYSIDE

I've lived in Australia all my life, but have never known more than a handful of Sheilas. Where does the idea of the average Australian woman being called Sheila come from?

Emma Saunders, Peregian Beach, Australia

This comes from a woman of high birth in the late ninteenth century called Sheila Sumstock-Caluminosumpter (pron. 'Cooper'), a woman who surpassed Queen Victoria, for whom she was a lady-in-waiting, in her grandeur and self-importance. She was married to the simpering Lord Granchild who was content to hole up in his Scottish castle for years on end working on his prototype for a long-distance communication device. He completed it a full ten years after Alexander Graham Bell's invention, so distracted by his work that he was told of the defeat by way of the castle's new telephone, which he had instinctively answered.

Unsatisfied by her spouse's retiring nature, Sheila made a celebrity of herself by her extravagant and passionate affairs with leading figures from the arts and sciences. Caruso vowed never to sing in London again after a weekend with her left him voiceless for a month, and later in life Freud used her as the basis for his controversial 'Hauteur Theory'.

In 1910, aged sixty, but with her much older husband showing no signs of fading (he would die aged 109 in 1936, of shock, on meeting his first black person), she changed her name to Simpson-Cooper and moved to Australia where she felt she could establish a social set from scratch and be at its centre. Things did not work out as planned. When she reached the colony she found people oblivious to high breeding, and the men enjoyed her confrontational style and could match her for effrontery. What's more, not a fortnight off the boat, she received a telegram telling her she was freshly divorced for the crime of abandonment, and cut off from her husband's coffers.

Making the best of things she established the most hygienic, expensive and well-stocked bordello in Sydney whose fame spread fast and wide. Men across the country would save up for a long-distance visit and it became a stock phrase that passed between Aussie soldiers in the First World War: 'We'll soon be back at Sheila's'.

She entered a serene old age and a kind of respectable infamy among Sydney society in the 1920s, popularity with returning troops having helped her to open three new whorehouses and a noodle bar. She died in the same year as her husband, surrounded by the offspring of her employees (whose education she funded) and just as the phrase Sheila began to come into general usage as an epithet for a friendly, simpatico or likeable female. Later it changed to something more offhand or (as used by non-Aussies) sarcastic and disparaging, but this is pure ignorance. It's much like the English way of referring to a woman as a 'bird', which comes from the Middle English 'brid' (meaning bride) – more a compliment than anything else.

Prof. Steve Dumughn, Department of Sexual History, Watford University

I think, therefore I am, are you?

Christophe Matricule, Lyons, France

This 'clever' reworking of Descartes' famous line, often misattributed to Jean-Paul Sartre, was actually the work of top advertising company Greeb, Greeb and Smock for the 1994 perfume '. . .' (pronounced by silently mouthing the word 'pretension' under one's breath).

'. . .' was a great success, made famous by Joe Pasquale's assertion on *Celebrity Family Fortunes* that he wears nothing but '. . .' in bed.

CHARLOTTE MEWS, ST DAVID'S, WALES

I'm afraid the line really is Sartre's, though controversy persists on whether he meant it as a cutting philosophical satire on the work of Descartes, or in reply to a letter from his little 'Beaver', Simone de Beauvoir.

De Beauvoir is known to have written to Sartre on 14 June 1942, asking whether he would be attending Albert Camus's drinks party in Les Deux Magots that evening. Sartre's Cartesian reply in the affirmative was wearisome, to say the least.

CHARLES D'AUTEUIL, MARSEILLES

Indeed the line is Sartre's, though it is better known in England for its appearance in Noël Coward's 1945 revue, 'Philosophical Love'. The closing song is recited by the two lovers, 'Jean-Pierre' and 'Segolène' (Sartre and de Beauvoir), by this stage of the performance 'hilariously' dressed in full black-and-white minstrel make-up:

I think, therefore I am, are you?
I dreamt of you the whole night through
And though my luck in love has passed
At les cartes I'm learning fast,
You can keep your Plato, Hume and old Camus

JEREMY TRUMP, REFORM CLUB, PALL MALL

Why have urban foxes become so much more daring in the last few years?

David Extant, Truro

I asked this the other week and got an extraordinarily full answer from my colleague Dr Chloe Healy, the octogenarian canine expert.

Apparently there was a village called Fassbinder in Germany which, in the Second World War, was evacuated so soldiers could practise for a foreign occupation – much as the Brits did, at the same time, with the village of Tyneham in Dorset. Within weeks stories of ghosts spread among the first garrison to be stationed there. Unbeknownst to the soldiers a nearby scientific institute had been given blanket funding to develop human intelligence in animals for military application. This facility, run by Dr Rudolph von Nietels (later the only man to be hanged *twice* at Nuremberg) did develop intelligent human-animal hybrids, most famously the dolphins that dragged mines towards Allied ships and, less well known, battalions of capuchin monkeys trained to imitate the 'characteristic movements' of Jews and provide target practice for companies of stormtroopers in the Black Forest.

A skulk of foxes [*He's right, Penny! I looked it up. Coll. noun for foxes: skulk, lead or leash. And you can have a kaleidoscope of butterflies. Isn't that CHARMING? Kettle on, please.*] proved useless, however, as the cunning attributed to those animals proved to be quite true.

Ingrained with human intelligence, they proved slyly selfish and pleasure-infatuated animals and were set free by von Nietels. Having set up residence in the nearby abandoned village of Fassbinder, they alarmed the credulous troops with their antics. Several soldiers broke down the door of an abandoned beerhall after sounds of smashing glass and saloon-style piano playing had been heard, to find a drunken group of foxes in smoking jackets, cigars in ashtray and brandy in glasses all round the table, a fifth (who had folded with a pair of sevens) stirring a huge pan of eggs rancheros on the stove. Another fox soon afterwards learned to thread film and work a projector, and soldiers in the thick of a full-scale freak-out tumbled onto the moonlit street a few days later to find an audience of randy foxes screeching to the sight of Marlene Dietrich in rapturous silver light against the church's stone wall.

Finally the authorities exterminated the vermin to prevent training being further hindered. The last fox to be killed was discovered in the tiny-windowed box room above the village's rectory, quill in hand, having amassed since his arrival the MS of the first four volumes of a magisterial *bildungsroman*. We have only the word of the one soldier who read it before it was consigned to the regimental bonfire, but his description whets the appetite. It told of the deprivation of an urban birth to a mother addicted to bratwurst stolen in mouldy globs from dustbins, the discovery of a mentor (his father being, in the manner of such families, absent) in a prematurely grey fox, who is eventually caught, in a very moving sequence, between lanes on the autobahn, and finally mown down by a Volkswagen. It told of his adolescent doubts over the gender of the foxes he felt attracted to, his first shy love beneath the fronded ferns of Hurtgen Forest, and his inclinations to write being met with indignation and ridicule by his fellow woodland creatures, only to find encouragement from a wise beaver with the technique of carving her poems on mudbanks with her tail. A troubled affair resulted from this, the soldier's diary tells us, but the novel is cut off at the point when she demands he learn to swim or leave her, and we are left hanging at the water's edge.

No similar animal-intelligence experiments were carried out by other societies after the war and our so-brief insight into the imaginations of our fellow creatures will now likely never be expanded. The anonymous fox author (shot, burned and shovelled into a stream) bequeaths literature only the title of his unfinished work: *The Fox of Life*.

D. BENSON, NEW YORK

What's the oldest trick in the book?

Phillipa Wall, Norwich

There's this thing I can do with the end of my knob when I've had a few pints – I sort of pull it while doing a handstand, and basically make Mickey Mouse's face. My mates think it's hilarious; I don't know if it's the oldest trick in the book, though??

TREVOR MIMS, BRISTOL

[Ed: I think it's relatively safe to say that Mr Mims's trick, while impressive, is not the oldest in the book. Penny, look behind you as you type this. Does it look like Mickey Mouse to you, dear girl?]

There are several candidates for this coveted title, but I would guess the answer is the sleight of hand shown by Ramses III, Pharaoh of Egypt, who can be observed in one hieroglyph pretending to take a baby's nose off, holding his thumb just so. It wasn't a very funny trick then, and it isn't very funny four thousand years later, but that never stopped our father.

WILLIAM AND TREVOR APHEX (CONJOINED), IDAHO

Why do houses carry signs saying 'SOLD'?

Marvin Gardens, East Ham

This is a matter of form. Like saying 'bless you' after a sneeze to protect the sneezer from the plague.

In the first days of estate-agentism in the seventeenth century it was a genteel art engaged in by the idiot sons of genteel families, the popular formula running (as recorded in a furious letter from John Donne to the incompetent

169

letting agent of his house in Mitcham) 'first son heir, second son lawyer, third son vicar, fourth son land agent unless inflicted with wit or soul in which case – writer, gaol, both, a hopeless future has hee'.

Donne made the best of being both a writer and a man of the cloth, though. When the Mitcham house failed to sell he wrote an especial ode which he pasted to a board and propped outside:

Oh doe not sell, for I shall hate
all houses so, when thou art gone.
That thee I shall not celebrate
When I remember, thou wast one
[It went on for two more verses]

The poem sold for forty guineas, but he never got an offer on the house, and there he lived until his death.

Knowing this story, Samuel Johnson took up this method, popularising the habit with his characteristic descriptions:

FOR SALE: Charming domicile in historic district, no more than two dozen floorboards broken or missing, health-giving draught. Available for lease or purchase at a price no less than £2 a week or £500 outright. Apply J. Boswell, same address.

OFFER IN: Reasonable, if not persuasive, from an unfortunate WHIG. Better offer from a right-thinking TORY welcomed for this important dwelling. Will accept £350.

SOLD: Blessedly to a wise Tory lady understanding that the Scots are an INFERIOR race and the plays of

GOLDSMITH sadly under-rated by a complacent public. Therefore happily accepted offer of £150.

By Dickens's time it was commonplace for estate agents to use signs to brag of the progress of their business ventures, as seen in *Bleak House* where Mr Truelove walks along the passages of Lincoln's Inn Fields and observes a pattern of signs with messages such as 'FOR LET – indigent family unable to sustain rent' and 'ACCEPTABLE RESIDENCE for a YOUNG FAMILY – tenant in last stages of illness'. Later in the novel an estate agent appears in the company of Mr Smallweed, toping in the Hunted Lion pub on Hope Street. He is seen to be

> *a tall thin man in clothes that inexpensively aped the style of a gentleman with no remarkable success, his eyes not choosing ever to meet those of his interlocutors and his face so pallid as to give an appearance of death that only his working mouth disproved. This mouth, formed by twin lips too thin for tailor's pencil to depict with a single stroke, gave birth to untruths with such regularity and conviction they caused passers-by to stop and wonder what common fact they could deny next. Should Smallweed declare 'It is Tuesday', they would produce an argument against that calendar truth unequalled in persuasiveness though the history of oration. Should Clitterbuck have the temerity to suggest that the sun would rise tomorrow, the letting agent would deliver a peroration of such force that it would have him begging forgiveness for his error. It had perhaps not occurred to either gentleman, while walking with him beside the river, to say, 'You are not drowned, sir!' and*

*to allow his pursuit of disproof to its satisfactory
conclusion. If it had, they were yet to act on it.*

It seems the modern estate agent can be said to have
existed by this era.

SIMON POTTER, WIMBLEDON

What's the perfect sandwich?

Tricia Gall, Bristol

Robbie Williams and a young Marlon Brando. Yum!

KENNETH PLEASURE, BRIGHTON

*[Ed note: check KP's handwriting, Penny. It's Plum, isn't it?
He's gone underground. Fetch my shotgun!]*

Is it just me, or have any other readers noticed that Pret Á
Manger, after the 'breadless sandwich' of last year, are now
selling *foodless* sandwiches in brightly packaged triangular
boxes? Surely that's going too far.

GEORGINA HOPKIN, GLASGOW

As a mother, I'm worried about the message being sent out to young girls by the 'foodless sandwich'. It just panders to the media frenzy over the 'size zero' debate . . . And now that the *Daily Mail* has uncovered the *minus 2* size scandal on the catwalks of Milan, where completely intangible models are projected onto a virtual backdrop, I just can't see the end of this. Soon we'll all cease to exist, and then who are Pret Á Manger going to sell their sandwiches to?

MARGARET SOUP, CHELTENHAM

I was listening to Garrison Keillor's radio show and a character referred to himself as a closet claustrophobe – is this possible?

Giovanni Bruno, Palermo

Of course, as the astronauts in the near-disastrous Apollo 11 mission found out. Only hours into the journey Neil Armstrong, who had withstood months of the most stringent psychometric testing and physical training, suffered a nervous fit and began asking for his mother. The crew calmed him down but he began to suffer delusions, claiming to be Louis Armstrong's brother and playing 'terrible dirges' (according to Michael Collins, the third astronaut) through an imaginary trumpet made from the hole formed by closing his forefinger and thumb. The real drama of the moon landing wasn't the lack of fuel or the dangerously small margin for error in landing and take-off from the moon, but preventing Armstrong from ripping open the thin fabric of the craft or distracting the others at crucial moments. He challenged them to arm wrestles, attempted to gain the controls and repeatedly started food fights with their limited supplies.

On landing he was allowed to step onto the moon first only because the other two were so sick of him – the broadcast footage was edited on a six-second delay by NASA staff to remove the sight of Edwin 'Buzz' Aldrin's hands shoving him through the hatch. Armstrong could barely contain his glee – if you listen again to his famous utterance, when he reaches the word 'mankind' he fluffs it and begins to giggle.

The last straw came when Aldrin and Collins found he had smuggled a golf club and balls on board and was content to pitch and putt across the lunar surface for a few days rather than gather samples. Waiting until he slept they sedated Armstrong and forcibly restrained him for the entire journey home.

RUPY BELMULLET, THROBE, SOMERSET

On the subject of phobias, I wonder if anyone else saw the fascinating interview with Prince Edward in this week's edition of *TV Quick*, in which he finally spoke out about his paralysing fear of bunting, which has made him a nervous wreck at public engagements since he was a child. Many columnists mocked Edward for squealing as his open-topped carriage wound its way through the crowds at Charles and Diana's wedding in the summer of 1981, but perhaps sympathy would have been more forthcoming if this genetic phobia had been more widely known at the time. His grand-father, George VI, famously stuttered when giving public orations, but should we not instead applaud the bravery of these men who were forced to spend their entire working lives at the mercy of the fluttering red, white and blue sharks' teeth looming from every street corner and clock tower?

JANICE BREADTH, WOKING

[Ed note: Perhaps other readers would like to write in with their strange phobias? Do send to us at the usual address. Penny: could you do me a favour, my dear? The work experience boy – the one with that awful 'hoodie' – has met with an unfortunate . . . accident. I keep the Winchester in excellent working order, as you know, but there you go; rifles will go off in one's hand if due care is not taken. Luckily he was standing on my crimson Turkish rug at the time, but even so, could you please arrange for Svetlana the cleaning lady to sort out the mess? There's a girl.]

W hich came first, the chicken or the egg?

Harold Bunflap, Krakow

Much hay is made of this question being unanswerable – not true. Archeology shows that forebears of the chicken (the squarp, thirteen million years; the Mesozoic

175

doubleneck rooster, seventeen million years; the twatfinch, twenty-two million years) gave birth to eggs rather than full-formed offspring. The egg came first.

PROF. HENRY HAMPTON, SMELLING, NORTH SUFFOLK

The chicken is well known as being directly descended from the red-crested marsh squatter, a land bird with two-centimetre legs and genetic incontinence (its evolutionary survival probably down to no other animal wanting to eat it). Fossils have shown a pregnant mother with full-grown infants in its belly. The chicken came first.

PROF. BRADLEY BROOK, SNIFFING, EAST SUFFOLK

How bitterly I watch Prof. Brook promulgating his foetid lies. He knows I'm on to him, the charlatan. I've seen the time-travel device he is building in his back garden to go back, plant evidence and prove himself right! Does he not know tampering with history could have disasterous effects? Think of the future, Brook!

PROF. HAMPTON, NORTH SUFFOLK

The learned professor may disagree with my theories, but in flinging bricks through my specially aluminium-framed orchid house he was taking matters too far. Hampton is now safe in the Aldeburgh Home for the Mentally Dispossessed. I hear he gets an egg for breakfast and chicken for dinner. So that should satisfy his view of the order of things at least.

PROF. BROOK, EAST SUFFOLK

It is not seemly for professors to argue in this way in front
of the public. You should make up with Henry and look at
why you were really arguing in the first place. Perhaps
because you are a little too interested in each other? Since
Digby and I got over our differences and learned to type
next to each other in bed without bickering, life has never
been so sweet. And the sex is great.

PROFS D. DUMBLE & H. H. UNSELF

What does it all mean?

Desmond Tutu, Republic of South Africa

According to the Venerable Bede:

> *The present life of man, O king, seems to me, in
> comparison of that time which is unknown to us, like
> to the swift flight of a sparrow through the room
> wherein you sit at supper in winter, with your
> commanders and ministers, and a good fire in the
> midst, whilst the storms of rain and snow prevail
> abroad; the sparrow, I say, flying in at one door, and
> immediately out at another, whilst he is within, is
> safe from the wintry storm; but after a short space of
> fair weather, he immediately vanishes out of your
> sight, into the dark winter from which he had*

emerged. So this life of man appears for a short
space, but of what went before, or what is to follow,
we are utterly ignorant.

This image of man's life – the flight of a sparrow through
the warmth and light of a great hall, and back out into the
blizzard – has troubled thinkers for centuries. What
depresses me is that in the Naughties, the cosy cheer of a
banqueting hall has been replaced by the local B&Q, where
I spend most of my Sundays buying bathroom fittings for
my buy-to-let; and all of the local sparrows have died out.
In fact, the only wildlife in Hackney is the rats. So here's
your updated Bede analogy: life is basically a rat running
through the wallpaper aisle of Halfords, and back out into
the rain.

TERESA BENTHAM, SOCIETY FOR THE POINTLESS PROMOTION OF
PESSIMISM

'It all' is a fairly straightforward construction which I would
expect to be comprehensible to even the most basic
English speaker. But, with standards of grammar slipping
ever lower, one should never be surprised at what people
need to have explained. 'It' is the singular form of the noun
indicating an asjkjckl lllllllllllllllllllllllllllllll

SIR PETER FROWNLOW, HASTINGS

I duly submit the last words of my father, who was found
slumped at his desk, over the keyboard of his faithful old
typewriter. He would have wanted me to send it in – he

loved writing letters to periodicals, even if they were about the topic of grammar, which he taught for forty years and which thoroughly, utterly bored him. In all other respects he was in good health. The coroner said he seemed to suffer a sudden, unexplained cardiac arrest, almost as if he spontaneously willed it.

BEATRICE FROWNLOW, HASTINGS

[Ed note: HAHA! So it IS possible to bore someone to death. I knew it. And there was I about to force you to read the Evening Standard *to test my theory, you poor wretch, Penny. Take the afternoon off, I feel victorious. Maybe a jaunt down to Buck Pal for the changing of the guard – can you check, has my restraining order expired yet, O angel of the office?]*

Who comes up with all those marketing sayings, e.g. 'thinking outside of the box'?

Garth Melting, Shrewsbury

Many such common phrases, from 'low-hanging fruit' to 'ducks in a row', have evolved quite naturally from the simple act of putting groups of gel-haired advertising wankers in an office and closing the door. This particular phrase derives from a common office 'joke' of the late 1980s in which work-experience juniors were blindfolded, locked up inside small metal boxes, and pushed down the stairs. Only those on the 'outside of the box' could be taken seriously as fee-earning high-flyers, while office juniors bumped and bruised by years 'inside the box' could only dream of the light and air of Executive Life. 'Thinking outside of the box', then, was all about being creative, successful, free. Somewhat darker was the famous sexual harassment case of 1988, where one of the bosses of marketing firm Sandham and Grey reportedly told his secretary that he had been 'thinking inside of her box'. He never worked again.

GUY SHINGLES, WHITSTABLE, KENT

So many of the glib, irritating phrases that bombard us from the billboards and advertising breaks have, in fact, come from some of our supposedly greatest minds. Salman Rushdie, for instance, came up with the Milk Marketing Board's 'Naughty . . . but nice!' slogan from the late seventies and we have no lesser mortal than Sigmund Freud to thank for another. As he submitted to the effects of gas anaesthetic before an operation on his mouth in 1934, he raved that he wanted to 'p-p-pick up a penguin'. One of the surgeons is said to have raised their eyebrows and, once the father of psychoanalysis was comatose, remarked, 'That was some Freudian slip!'

The phrase 'thinking outside of the box' in advertising terms may originate in office bullying tactics from the 1980s, but it was first used much, much earlier, during the worst days of the emasculation cult of frightful Chinese Jin Dynasty ruler Lam Su (whose reign of terror has been incorrectly attributed to her predecessor, Tzu Lam, in many history books). She is said to have lived in a silver palace decorated with the genitalia of a hundred peasant slaves, who, now eunuchs, lay down to form a human carpet for her to walk on. When she crossed a river a raft would be assembled from the quivering flesh of a dozen weeping men. During these great purges she amassed an almost limitless wealth as no male army would fight her hordes of women carrying Chinese xiudong (literally, 'crotch weapon' – it resembles a modern potato peeler). Her linguistic bequest comes to us from the legend of her death, when, challenged by an itinerant soothsayer to prove she was invincible, she had a human coffin made and was buried alive in it, proclaiming, 'I, Lam Su, am eternal! I shall THINK myself out of the box!' But the soothsayer was in fact an exiled prince who, conspiring with her ladies-in-waiting, had arranged that the box be made out of men who had *not* been castrated. She was duly lowered into the ground, and fucked to death.

AVERY GOLDMINE, MINNESOTA

Is correct spelling and grammar really that important?

M. Ismail Khogyani, Samoa

Orthography, grammar, and syntax are tremendously important, a fact borne out by a tragic misreading on my part. In response to an advert in the shop window of my

181

local butcher's, I took my prized Pomeranian poodle, Ralph, along to an address in the next village, glad for the help. I am just a poor old woman, and have long since stopped giving Ralph the exercise she deserves. The advert itself – it transpired – was entirely honest in its intentions; the fault was entirely in my misreading of a single letter: 'I will walk your dog. Call *******'. Poor Ralph!

MRS LEONARD BEACHAM, SOMERSET

I can sympathise entirely with Mrs Beecham and her ordeal with Ralph the dog. Readers may remember a certain Tory shadow minister's notorious interview with *Hello!* magazine earlier this year, for which he was immediately sacked by David Cameron. The tirade as it appeared in the audio tape of the interview is as follows:

> *They're parasites these 'Wives or Girlfriends', make no mistake about that. They do nothing to contribute to our economy, strolling around naked in hot countries like savages before returning to Britain, strolling around with their smug, garishly painted 'Wife or Girlfriend' faces, relying on handouts rather than working for a living. They make me sick.*

The honourable gentleman's mistake was a small one – it is, of course, Wives AND Girlfriends, or 'WAGS' – but he surely cannot be blamed for *Hello!*'s decision to reproduce his mistake when typing out the acronym in print.

JEEVES WORCESTER, PELHAM

Is correct spelling and grammar really that important?

[Ed note: Penny? No one's pointed out that the moronic questioner means 'Are correct spelling and grammar important'? I resign. You can take over. Sorry I've been so beastly to you over the years, dear Penny. I always knew it. Our readership: intellectual ants and arseholes to a man. Oh and last thing: do correct 'Clarfications' would you, there's a good girl.]

End note: If any of our esteemed readers have burning questions – especially about the life of Queen Victoria – that they would like answered, please send them in to us c/o penny@oldgitmagazine.co.uk